The Share Book
Rosemary Burr

With an introduction by –
The Prime Minister, **Margaret Thatcher**

Published by ROSTERS LTD.
60 Welbeck Street, London W1

First edition 1985
Reprinted 1985
© Rosemary Burr
ISBN 0-948032-10-3

Printed and bound by
Cox & Wyman Ltd, Reading.

1O DOWNING STREET

THE PRIME MINISTER

I am delighted to be able to introduce <u>The Share Book.</u>

Throughout the country, men and women are taking a new interest in the stock market. The number of shareholders is growing for the first time in decades. There is a new recognition, both in the City and elsewhere, of the importance of the individual investor.

I welcome these changes. Wider share ownership means that more people can have a stake in British industry and commerce, and can share in its success. And I am proud to be part of a Government that has helped bring all this about.

We have made special efforts, as part of our privatisation policy, to aim offers of Government shares at the individual investor. We have done away with the investment income surcharge, halved stamp duty and raised the Capital Gains Tax threshold sixfold. All of this helps to reduce the burden on the private shareholder. It is my fervent wish that new investors will continue to be attracted to the stock market, and that those who have recently bought shares for the first time will want to buy more.

For too long the world of stocks and shares has been a mystery understood only by a small minority. Yet the new opportunities will go begging unless enough people know how to take advantage of them. Now, at last, the tide is turning, and I am sure that this book will contribute to this process. It is about the nuts and bolts of buying, holding and selling shares. It should prove a valuable source of information and advice for many.

Margaret Thatcher

<u>OCTOBER 1985</u>

CONTENTS

Section One

Section I

Chapter One
Starting Out

If you are new to the world of shares then there are a few basic principles it is essential to get under your belt before you are let loose on a buying spree. When you put your money in a bank, you are called a depositor. In return for using your money to lend to other people at a profit the bank will agree to pay you interest and repay your money on request. When you put money into a company, the rules are rather different. You are known as a shareholder and actually own part of the business. As a shareholder you are entitled to receive a part of the company's profits in direct proportion to the size of your shareholding. The directors who run the company are responsible for its day-to-day management. They have a legal duty to keep you informed about their actions and the company's progress. The amount you earn on your investment will ultimately depend on the skill of the directors.

Return on Shares

There are two ways you can earn a return on your shares. First, you can make a capital profit by selling your shares for more than they cost you. Second, you can receive an income. As a shareholder you are entitled to receive dividends each year. Depending upon the success of the company and its future need for cash the directors will set aside a sum of money to be distributed among shareholders according to the size of their holdings. This dividend will be a fixed amount per share and in growing companies should increase regularly each year.

There are no guarantees either about the level of dividends or the price you will be paid for your shares. So why give up the security of knowing how much you will earn on a building society deposit for the risks involved in shares? The answer is simple – in the hope of earning a higher return.

Past Performance

Using past performance as a guide, investors who simply left their money on deposit with a bank or building society over the last ten years have failed to even match inflation. That means their spending power has decreased over the years and their savings are worth less than when they started. If you had £1,000 on 1st January 1975, it would have needed to treble to £3,000 by 1st January 1985, merely to keep pace with inflation. In fact, over that ten year period a bank deposit would have grown to £1,759 and a building society deposit to £2,139.

Partly in response to these sort of statistics the Thatcher government has introduced a range of what are called index-linked investments. These are investments which guarantee to provide savers with not only their money back intact, but adjusted fully to match inflation as measured by the Retail Prices Index. These index-linked vehicles provide a useful option for those investors simply wishing to maintain the real value of their savings, but do not provide a chance to substantially increase their money.

Importance of Timing

For those interested in not simply maintaining the value of their savings but increasing it, then some form of investment in shares is the answer. The actual return on any individual shareholding will depend upon the company whose shares you buy and particularly crucial when you decide to buy and sell. For example, take the case of two investors in British Telecom. Mr Lucky was allotted 500 shares when the government first sold them in November 1984 at 50p and sold his shares for 160p in May 1985, netting a cosy profit of £550 equal to 220%. Mr Bodger, on the other hand, bought British Telecom shares at 200p in June 1985 and sold them for 180p a month later, resulting in a loss of 10%.

International Record

That said, it is worth examining the overall trend in share prices over the past ten years. Stockbrokers Phillips & Drew provide some useful international data comparing the returns in percentage terms if you had invested in the biggest 11 stock markets in the world. The figures show on average investors in the UK market would have enjoyed a 31.7% annual return between 1975 and 1984. However, this average figure is rather misleading as an overall indicator as the starting point in 1975 was at a historically low level following the 1974 share slump. If the figures are reworked starting in 1976 then the average return falls slightly.

Equities: Annual returns in local currencies

% pa	1975	1976	1977	1978	1979	1980	1981	1982	1983	1984	Ave 75–84
USA	37.3	23.7	−7.3	6.6	18.6	32.6	−5.0	21.6	22.6	6.2	14.8
Japan	19.2	21.4	−3.1	26.0	4.2	9.5	17.3	6.0	25.2	26.4	14.8
UK	152.0	2.2	49.1	8.5	11.4	35.4	13.7	29.2	29.1	31.9	31.7
Canada	18.3	9.2	6.2	30.6	50.6	24.0	−10.7	6.5	33.8	−1.4	15.4
Germany	41.8	−3.9	12.2	9.7	−7.4	4.0	4.9	19.4	44.2	11.2	12.5
Australia	57.5	3.8	6.7	21.2	49.5	45.0	−20.2	−10.7	70.3	−4.8	18.1
Switzerland	46.0	3.2	5.4	−1.4	10.4	2.9	−8.1	14.8	30.4	5.9	10.0
France	46.1	−11.4	0.2	53.9	24.3	10.7	−10.2	14.9	68.0	23.2	19.4
Singapore	70.8	12.7	0.4	34.6	28.7	56.9	15.8	−14.1	32.7	−24.9	17.9
Netherlands	61.8	7.0	7.7	4.7	15.4	27.2	−0.4	24.7	61.0	29.6	22.2
Hong Kong	118.6	30.5	−12.4	23.2	88.6	79.7	−7.0	−36.6	16.8	47.8	26.6

Source: Phillips & Drew.

As you can see from the table there are some menacing minuses lurking to trap the unwary. This only serves to underline the point that shares are volatile. Share prices tend to dance around rather than moving in straight lines.

However, over the long term the movement in prices has been steadily upwards, even allowing for major collapses such as 1974. As you can see from the table, Hong Kong has been one of the best markets to invest in over the past decade, but it has thrown up losses in three out of those ten years.

The message to learn from this mass of statistics is that in the long term, an investment in shares should out-perform leaving your money on deposit, provided you spread your money around a representative sample of stocks. In the short term, however, you should not be surprised to see some price falls. It is this very volatility of price which provides short term trading and longer term buying opportunities for investors. In retrospect the best time to have bought shares would have been the tail end of the 1974 share price slump and he worst at the end of 1975 after the market had bounced sharply back. But no-one can consistently get their timing right. When buying shares, as with investments in general, it pays not to be too greedy. After all, paper profits cannot pay bills. Remember the only genuine profit is the one you have banked.

Chapter Two
Types of Stocks & Shares

Before deciding where to channel your money it is worth coming to grips with the various ways you can invest. This is essential as the potential profit or loss will vary depending upon your choice. Normally you will be considering buying the ordinary shares in a company, but there may be other types of share or stock available. There are five key factors to ponder:–

    1. How safe is it?
    2. Am I investing in the company or lending it money?
    3. Is my income fixed or variable?
    4. Will I have the chance to make a capital gain?
    5. What is the tax position?

Ordinary Shares
Safety: The share price will depend upon the company's fortunes, market perception of the Company and overall trends in the stock market. In the event of the company going bust, ordinary shareholders are at the tail-end of the cash queue.

Status: Equity investment.

Income: Paid in the form of dividends fixed by the directors twice a year.

Capital: Prospect of either capital gain or loss depending upon share price movement after your purchase.

Tax: Dividends are paid net of standard rate tax. Non-tax-payers can reclaim the tax paid on their behalf. Higher rate taxpayers will have an extra tax bill. Small investors are unlikely to face a capital gains tax bill. For the year 1985-86 the first £5,900 of capital gains are tax free.

Variation: A few companies have two types of ordinary shares, voting and non-voting. It is usually best to buy the voting shares.

Preference Shares

Safety: The share price will depend upon the same factors as applied to ordinary shares. However, preference shares are marginally safer than ordinary shares and tend to be less volatile. The reason for this is two-fold. In the event of the company going bust, preference shareholders rank ahead of ordinary shareholders in the queue for repayments and the yield on the shares is usually higher.

Status: Equity investment.

Income: Paid in the form of dividends fixed by the directors twice a year.

Capital: Prospect of either capital gain or loss depending upon share price movement after your purchase.

Tax: Dividends are paid net of standard rate tax. Non-tax-payers can reclaim the tax paid on their behalf. Higher rate taxpayers will have an extra tax bill. Small investors are unlikely to face a capital gains tax bill. For the year 1985-86 the first £5,900 of capital gains are tax free.

Variations: You may also come across redeemable prefer-ence shares. This means that the company has the option to buy back the shares at a price stated at the outset. Before buying redeemable preference shares it is essential to find out the price at which the company has agreed to repurchase the shares and also try to discover whether it is likely that the shares will in fact be repurchased in the near future. A company will only buy the shares back if it has unused cash available, or if it is able to raise money more cheaply elsewhere.

Cumulative redeemable preference shares provide investors with an extra degree of security. If the company is unable to pay dividends on the shares in any one year then this missed payment is carried forward to the next year. This process can be repeated as many times as is necessary.

Convertible preference shares are a halfway house between preference shares and ordinary shares. They are preference shares which also give the holder the option to switch or convert their holding into the ordinary shares at a fixed price over a certain period. They can be a useful each way bet on a company's fortunes for the more conservative investor. You can enjoy the greater security of being a preference shareholder and a chance to enjoy any substantial rise in the price of the ordinary shares. Make sure you check the fine print on the conversion terms and the existing ordinary share price before buying.

Warrants

Safety: A warrant is a piece of paper issued by a company entitling the owner to buy shares in that company at a certain price. The warrant only has a value if people are prepared to buy it now in the hope that at a later date the company's share price will be higher than the price at which warrant holders can buy its shares. It is a high risk way of investing in a company.

Status: Equity investment.

Income: None.

Capital: Potential for huge gains or losses.

Tax: Capital gains tax is payable if gains exceed annual allowance.

Loan Stock

Safety: Reasonably safe. The company will have stated a date by or on which it intends to repay the loan. If a company goes bust, loan stock holders leapfrog both preference and ordinary shareholders in the cash queue.

Status: Unsecured loan.

Income: Paid in the form of interest fixed at the time the

12

stock is issued. This means you can work out in advance how much income you will receive on your investment.

Capital: There are two ways of making a capital gain, either because the price of the stock in the market rises or because you buy the stock at below its issue price and wait for the company to repay the loan.

Tax: Interest is paid net of standard rate tax. Capital gains tax is only payable if your gains exceed the stated amount per year, currently £5,900 for 1985-86.

Variations: Convertible loan stock gives the holder the option to buy ordinary shares at a fixed price on a certain date. As with convertible preference shares it provides a rather safer route into the riskier ordinary shares while providing a higher income than on the shares. Again, check the terms at which you will be allowed to switch into shares and the current ordinary share price. The price of loan stock with a conversion option will be more volatile than the traditional loan stock, as part of its price will reflect the market's view of the value of the share option.

Debenture

Safety: Very safe. This is a loan secured against a stated asset such as property. Provided the asset is correctly valued and can be sold at a price at least equal to its valuation then debenture holders will be repaid in full.

Status: Secured loan.

Income: Fixed at the outset. Usually lower than the return on the unsecured loan stock.

Capital: There is unlikely to be room for sizeable gains or losses, although potential losses can occur in the short term or if you buy the stock above par and hold it until the company repays.

Tax: Income tax at your current band is payable on interest received. Capital gains tax may be due if your gains exceed the annual allowance.

The Risk Spectrum

Minimal	Debentures
Low	Loan Stock
Medium	Preference shares

13

| High | Ordinary shares |
| *Very high* | Warrants |

Government Securities

Safety: Very safe.

Status: Loan guaranteed to be repaid by Her Majesty's Government at par on or by a fixed date.

Income: Fixed at the time of issue. So you can work out your income in advance.

Capital: If you buy the stock below par then you can make a capital gain either by waiting until the government repays its loans or if the price rises, normally as a reflection of lower interest rates elsewhere. If you buy the stock at above par you are limiting your potential for capital gain.

Tax: Income tax is payable on interest received but capital gains are tax free if the gilt has been held for more than a year. When a gilt is sold within a year there is a potential capital gains tax liability. From 2nd July 1986, capital gains tax on gilts will be removed.

Variation: Index-linked gilts were introduced in 1982 by the Thatcher government. Instead of being repaid at par, the stock is repaid at face value adjusted to take account of any rise or fall in the retail price index since the stock was issued. So for instance, say the government issued £10m worth of index-linked stock 2000 2% in 1990 and that the retail price index rises by 20% between 1990 and 2000 then the government will repay each holder of £100 stock with £120. In the meantime, holders will receive £2 for each £100 stock in interest each year. The only people who will enjoy the index-linking in full are those who bought the stock on day one and held it to maturity.

Anyone considering buying index-linked gilts should be careful to do their sums thoroughly and it is probably best to seek expert counsel first. Most major stockbrokers will work out the return based on the current price and future projection for inflation. If you do anticipate a return to an era of roaring inflation then they are well worth investigating in greater detail.

Chapter Three
Where Shares are Traded

Now that you've mastered the basics about the range of stocks and shares available, the next crucial step is to discover where these are traded. This is vitally important as it will give you several clues about the status of the company, the volatility of its share price and how easy it will be to sell your shares.

Listed Company

Before a company can sell its shares on the stock market it must be thoroughly wetted by the Stock Exchange. This is to make sure it is financially sound and well managed. Collectively these requirements are referred to as the listing rules. Once a company has passed these tests with flying colours its shares may be listed, quite literally added to the Official List of shares traded on the London Stock Exchange.

The basic listing requirements are a five year track record and that 25% of the company's equity must be sold. From this you can tell that the company is reasonably well established and that there should be no shortage of supply in its shares which should ensure a smooth market without aritificially inflated prices.

Shareholders are further protected by the Stock Exchange reserving the right to halt or suspend dealings in a company's shares. This will only be done if it seems that a false market is developing in a company's shares. Defining a false market is difficult but broadly speaking the aim is to put all shareholders on an equal footing with access to the same news about a company. Typically a company's shares will be suspended if news of a takeover or financial reconstruction leaks out before the directors have made a formal announcement. Once the news is publicly known, dealings in the shares will be restarted.

When shares in a company are listed on another exchange, which in turn decides to suspend the quotation, then dealings in the shares will also be halted in London.

Unlisted Companies

Companies which cannot meet the requirements of a full listing may opt to join the Unlisted Securities Market. In order to qualify as an 'unlisted' company certain key rules must be met and the company itself will be equally thoroughly vetted as if it were applying for a full listing. The requirements are a three year trading record, and an undertaking to sell at least 10% of the company. There is no minimum size requirement.

As Unlisted Securities Market companies tend to be newer and smaller in size the risks and rewards may be greater. Much depends upon the individual company, it could be an old family firm which in theory would be able to comply with the full listing requirements but where the owners only wish to part with 10% of the business.

In July 1985 there were 299 companies traded on the USM varying in size from £200,000 to £179.9m. Since the market was launched in November 1980, 44 companies have graduated to a full listing, 15 have been taken over and seven re-organised.

As only 10% of a company's shares are available it may be more difficult to deal in USM shares than those of fully listed companies. The share price can be more volatile and just one sale or purchase can move the price by several percentage points, whereas a buy or sell order for say a million ICI shares would leave the price unchanged.

How the USM has Grown

Year	Number of Companies	Turnover
1980	23	£52.2m
1981	86	£282.2m
1982	136	£619.6m
1983	204	£1,226.3m
1984	268	£1,469.2m

Rule 535(3)

This category is for mineral exploration companies, which because they have no profits record are unable to qualify for a full listing. In all other respects they meet the standards laid down for quoted companies.

Rule 535(2)

This covers dealing in companies whose shares are not listed but where shareholders wish to conclude arms-length bargains usually for tax purposes.

Over-the-Counter

This is a market in shares run by licensed dealers in securities. There are no legal requirements which have to be satisfied and the market is completely unregulated. When the new legislation on the financial services industry is introduced in 1986 this regulatory vacuum is likely to be filled.

Until then investors should proceed with extreme caution as otherwise they could find themselves the proud owner of a worthless share certificate. Potential problems arise not just because there are no formal rules similar to the stock exchange's listing requirements but also because the functions of the jobber and stockbroker are rolled into one. This creates a huge temptation to turn into virtual share pushers. If a dealer is left with a sizeable amount of stock he may be tempted to ring a client and recommend purchases. Some investors have found that after succumbing to such blandishments they have been unable to sell their shares.

One licensed dealer, Granville & Co, only arranges matched bargains. That is it acts solely as a go-between. If you wish to sell some shares then a willing buyer will be found and the two transactions paired.

Unquoted

Shares in an unquoted company are not traded. If you do buy shares in such a company, either for an investment or perhaps as part of a profit sharing scheme, you will only be able to sell them if you can find a buyer and haggle over a price.

Securities Quoted Abroad

Stock Exchange members can deal in any stocks or shares listed on a recognised foreign exchange. If the share is not fully listed but is traded on the equivalent of our junior Unlisted Securities Market, members may also conclude transactions in these stocks.

Chapter Four
Figuring out Companies

Before you invest in a company it is well worth establishing a routine check up.

1. Look at the current price and see how this compares to the share's trading record over the past year. Most quality newspapers will quote yesterday's price and the high and low either for the calendar year or last twelve months. Compare this to the experience of other companies in the same sector and the market as a whole. From this you will know whether you are considering a high flier or a tortoise.

2. Find out how much shareholders are currently receiving by the way of dividends. This will feature alongside the price information about the company under the heading gross yield. The yield on a share is worked out as a percentage. It is the amount of dividends in pence divided by the share price in pence, multiplied by one hundred. It is called gross yield as it is calculated on the amount of dividends a company pays out rather than their value

after tax in the hands of standard rate taxpayers. Again you can compare the gross yield for all the companies in the sector and for the market as a whole.

3. Try to assess how safe the dividend payment is. Obviously it is no good picking a share with an above average yield only to discover that the company is cutting the dividends next time around. The key figure here is to be found under the column entitled 'cover', abbreviated to 'c'vr'. If a company has exactly enough spare cash after tax and interest at current profit levels to pay the stated level of dividends then the cover will be one. If it has three times as much then it will be three and if it could only afford to pay out half the stated level of dividends then the cover would be 0.5. So this statistic gives you a good idea of how safe your yield is and whether there is scope for a rise in dividends. Remember it is based on the most recent full year profit figures and can change dramatically with alterations in the company's trading fortunes.

4. Check the p/e. The short-hand for price earnings ratio. This is a way of relating a company's existing earnings capacity to its share price. It is calculated by dividing the earnings per share into the share price. Let's say a company's shares were at 10p. Following a disastrous year when profits were hit after lightning destroyed all its stock, it announced a huge leap in earnings per share from 1p to 6p. What will have happened to the p/e? Well, to begin with the p/e was $10/1 = 10$. Then it falls to $10/6 = 1.66$. On a p/e of 10 it will take a company ten years to generate earnings per share equal to the share price at current profit levels, while on a p/e of 1.66 it will only take the company about twenty-one months. If investors think a company's profits are growing very fast they will go on buying the shares and increasing the size of the p/e. Returning to the first example, the average p/e for a company in this sector could be 6. On the basis of earnings per share of 6p the shares would rate as a buy up to 36p $(6 \times 6p)$.

When assessing p/e's it is important to compare the figures for other companies in the same sector and look at this statistic in relation to other factors such as yield, cover and price history.

Where to Find the Information
The Stock Exchange publishes daily, weekly and monthly Official Lists. This is the only comprehensive guide to share prices of the approximately 7,000 quoted stocks and shares. It will give details of both the price jobbers were prepared to buy and sell shares and also indicate the number of transactions completed in a share.

The quality national dailies publish lists of share prices and details of dividends, yields, p/e's and cover. However, this only covers a small selection of companies who are prepared to pay for this information to be printed. Just because a company's share price is published in the paper does not mean it is a better or worse investment than a company which has decided not to pay to have its prices published. Unlike the Stock Exchange Official List, the newspapers publish what are called middle prices, halfway between the jobbers buying and selling price. As the newspapers go to print at different times in the day you can sometimes find a discrepancy between the published prices for the same company.

When you want to compare the figures for an individual company with a sector or the market as a whole then you will need to turn to the Financial Times. It publishes this information each day for a representative group of 739 shares known as the FT-All Share Index and also for 40 sectors of the market. It is located at the foot of the page headed London Stock Exchange, which also includes a daily market report of major share rises and falls.

Company Report and Accounts
To put some flesh on these bare statistical bones, you should take a look at the company's report and accounts. This is a legal document published each year about eight weeks after a group has announced its final results. Each report starts with a statement from the directors summarising the pattern of trading over the past year and outlining the company's

future prospects. A profit and loss account shows the results of the company's trading over the year. There is also a balance sheet at year-end which provides a snap-shot of the company's finances on a specific date. Plus a statement on funding, showing how the company finances its business and finally a paragraph from the accountants stating that all the information is correct.

Points to watch:–

1. Profits record.
2. Dividend record.
3. Indications of future expansion, compare figures for work in progress.
4. Changes in management.
5. Restructuring.
6. Changes in business activities.
7. Chairman's statement on future outlook.
8. Assets.
9. Bank overdraft.

Stockbroker

The large City brokers have full-time analysts researching many of the country's biggest quoted companies. They will visit companies and prepare reports assessing the growth and profits prospects. On the basis of these forecasts they will work out potential for rise in dividends and reformulate p/e's. If you are interested in buying shares in a company check to see if your broker can supply you with an up-to-date report.

Newspapers

As well as statistical information keep your eyes pinned to the financial sections of the papers for news which might affect the company's share price. This could be an item specifically relating to the company such as a contract or new shareholder, alternatively it may be news which will affect the industry in which it operates such as oil price fluctuations or the exchange rate movements.

Chapter Five
Choosing Shares: Investment Strategies

Never forget that when you buy shares you are actually investing in people, from the directors through to the office cleaner. You are showing your faith in their ability to generate growing profits.

Management

The quality of the company's management is absolutely critical. You should try to find out as much as possible about their track record, background, former companies where they worked, strengths and weaknesses.

Your stockbroker should be able to help fill in some of the details, a rummage through old library cuttings is another source and of course the report and accounts will show the company's track results over several years.

Ideally, you should look for depth of management, stability of senior staff and flair in the top echelons. For long term investors I would steer clear of companies whose current share price is supported solely on the basis of a handful of personalities who could move to their competitors at a moment's notice. Advertising and marketing companies are particularly prone to move-itis.

Management depth can become a critical factor as a company starts to expand. Without sound financial and administrative systems entrepreneurial companies can come a cropper. Several high technology companies or those involving products invented by the top directors are particularly vulnerable in this area. On the other hand companies with well trained and loyal staff should be able to motor virtually on there own steam, leaving the directors free to develop long term strategies.

Assets

Another crucial element to assess is the company's assets. These consist in a range of plant, machinery, property, investments, stock and cash. The key figure here is net assets per share. Net in this sense means after deducting a sum to pay off the company's creditors, debts and loans. Many company's report and accounts will include a figure for net assets per share but it is quite easy to work out for yourself. Simply divide the number of shares in issue into the total net assets. If there are various classes of shares you may need help in working out the sums.

The importance of the net asset per share is that it acts as a natural floor to support the share price. What it tells you in effect is how much each shareholder would be given if the company was shut up and its assets sold at the value given in the report and accounts. Don't take the figures in the report and accounts for granted, but go through them yourself and see whether you need to make any adjustments. Make sure you read all the small print, particularly the notes to the accounts.

Let's work through the typical assets of a company. First cash, no need to worry about the sum being wrong but remember a company with large amounts of cash will earn more when interest rates are high and less as rates fall. Second, shareholdings in other companies. If the company whose shares are purchased is quoted you can find a price and work out the current value of this stake. Plant and machinery. These are very difficult to value and in declining industries such as steel and textiles may have no resale value except for scrap. Stock. Again a thorny problem. Stock is only worth what it is sold for and many high tech companies have had to wipe huge sums off their assets for outmoded stock. Property. Most companies do not have up-to-date valuations of their property and many a sound investment has been based on uncovering potentially profitable developments hidden away in retail trading companies.

In general terms, provided the company is making reasonable profits and is not in a dying industry you cannot go far wrong by buying shares which are priced below the net asset per share. Such companies tend to pay relatively high yields. They should be regarded as medium term investments – either the existing management will start to make the assets sweat or the company is likely to be on the receiving end of a takeover bid. Shareholders win both ways.

Earnings

Many people argue that today prices simply reflect nothing more or less than a company's earnings. Although earnings are important, they need to be considered within the context of a company's management and assets.

Newcomers to the stock market may be surprised at the number of price rises and falls in a single share. This is because investors are constantly weighing up the latest news and comparing various companies at different price levels to see which rates as the best bargain. The market tends to react ahead of the events and in most cases the current year's earnings are marked into the company's share price. This means that it is very rare for a company's share price to rise sharply even after a better than expected set of results. If you notice a sharp price rising and then discover the company's figures are due to be announced in a few days it is probably too late to start buying.

The downside on the earnings element can be quite considerable. If you can see a profit in a share in an industry where there has been an announcement of earnings fall for a major company, you would do well to realise your gain. The market is not kind to sectors which go out of favour and prices can be slashed across a whole range of similar companies in just a few days. Such wholesale snips in share prices can throw up useful bargains as sentiment nearly always swings back at least part of the way.

Income

For new investors and those who like to play safe, shares with above average yields, known as income stocks, are worth investigating in depth. They tend to be less volatile in price and provided the company's earnings are sufficient to pay out a growing sum of dividends then they reduce the amount of risk in buying shares.

You will not receive as much income from shares as you would from a building society deposit but you will gain both the chance of a growing income and a capital profit. Don't just go for the share which is yielding the largest amount, especially if it is much higher than the rest. There may well be a good reason, for example if the market thinks the company will announce a cut in dividends.

Some companies offer their shareholders special concessions, known as perks or freebies. If you take the savings involved into account you can effectively boost your return from the shares in an extremely tax efficient way as there is no income tax payable on most discounts.

Growth

Growth stocks pay less than average in dividends but hold out the promise of rapid expansion in the future. They tend to be more volatile and subject to the whims of fashion that their cousins income stocks. The greater the distance between the company's current earnings capacity per share and its share price the higher the risk.

The best time to take money out of growth stocks is before they have been discovered by everyone else. Jumping on the bandwagon once a company price has risen dramatically can prove foolhardy as even the most vigorous company would find it impossible to expand its earnings by 40 times in the next couple of years.

Small Companies

The reason for investing in small companies is basically two fold: growth prospects and superior earnings power. Many smaller companies are traded on the Unlisted Securities Market and prices can prove very volatile. In a rising market they speed ahead but in a falling market at the first sign of people wanting to sell out the share price might drop like a stone. On the other hand the household names of the future are likely to be somewhere among the also rans, so it is a matter of doing your homework very thoroughly.

Penny Shares

Originally this term was used for shares worth less than 10p. They were basically equivalent to a bet on a 1000 to 1 horse. When a company was on the verge of going under its share price would slump to just a few pence. Now, however, the phrase has been widened to cover shares in all sorts of companies where these are priced at less than 50p or even a pound. The actual share price of a company is not important. What is essential is the yield, price/earnings ratio plus all the non-statistical aspects such as management flair.

Defensive Stocks

These tend to be shares with high yields which grow at fairly even but rather pedestrian speeds year in year out, come what may. Even if the country dives into recession people still smoke, drink, eat, play bingo, bet and buy clothing. So brewery companies, tobacco companies, fast food chains and some leisure stocks are defensive.

Recovery Stocks

These are shares in companies which have been badly hit, usually by a downturn in the economy. Traditionally they include textiles, engineering and builders. Before buying shares in such companies do check that you are not investing in a dying industry. Some companies may never recover their former glory and their future success will depend upon the management's skill in identifying new areas of business activity.

Chapter Six
Where to Buy Shares

Now that you've decided which shares to buy, how do you go about it? Unfortunately it is rather more complicated than just popping down to the local supermarket for the week's groceries. There are strict regulations in this country about who can buy and sell shares direct to the public.

Under the current law enshrined in the Prevention of Fraud Investment Act (1958) only three categories of people can sell shares to the public. These are stockbrokers, licensed dealers in securities and so-called exempt institutions. The exempt institutions include high street banks, merchant banks and members of the National Association of Security Dealers and Investment Managers (Nasdim), the self-regulatory body run by members of the investment industry.

The Stock Exchange regulates the activities of the stock-broking community. It sets minimum levels of competence and endeavours to uphold high standards of integrity among its members. Licensed dealers in securities are regulated either by the Department of Trade or Nasdim which vet the applicants to ensure they are fit and proper people.

It is essential at the outset to establish which type of institution is conducting your share business. Your choice will affect both the cost of the transaction itself and your ability to seek redress if anything untoward happens.

The Choice

First let's look at stockbrokers. At the moment brokers charges are fixed and every broker will bill its clients for the same fee or commission on most transactions. Smaller deals and those in so-called short dated government securities with a maturity of five years or less may be priced at the brokers' discretion. If the broker goes bust leaving you out of pocket then there is a well established procedure which rolls into motion. The Stock Exchange Compensation Fund is designed to ensure that customers of a member firm which fails to settle its obligations are repaid in full.

Second, licensed dealers in securities. There is no system of fixed commissions. Often you will see advertisements in the paper from such dealers offering to buy or sell shares free of commission. The important point to remember before leaping at such offers is that they may not be the bargains they seem. Be careful to check the prices at which the licensed dealer is proposing to conclude your business with the cost of dealing through a stockbroker. There is no compensation fund in place if the dealer should run into financial difficulties. Nasdim is working on a fund to cover its members while dealers licensed by the Department of Trade must inform new clients of any negligence insurance they have purchased. If you have any general complaints find out who has granted the dealer a license and write to the appropriate authority.

Third, the exempt category is a mixed bundle but again there is no compensation fund to provide share buyers with a safety net. Do note that although bank depositers are protected up to a fixed amount if a bank goes bust the scheme known as the Deposit Protection Scheme does not cover bank clients who have bought shares and may be out of pocket. On the question of charges, it is a matter of shopping around. Some merchant banks will deal in a limited number of pre-selected stocks free of commission to existing customers, mostly large institutions dealing in orders of several thousand pounds. Several of the high street banks now add their own charges on top of the standard stock-broking fees, as the table shows. On larger orders some banks waive this additional fee, while Lloyds Bank offers customers the choice of two different charging structures. Either the customer agrees that the bank will divide the commission with the broker and then pay £5 extra or the customer opts to pay the bank £10 and to let the broker keep all the commission. Normally it works out cheaper if you tell the bank to give all the commission to the broker as the over-all commission rate is lower in this instance.

Extra Charges on Share Transactions

High Street Bank	Cost*
Bank of Scotland	No extra charge
Barclays	Below £1,500 – £5 + VAT Over £1,500 – no extra charge
Lloyds	£5 on deals up to £20,000
Midland	Below £1,500 – £5 + VAT Over £1,500 – no extra charge
National Westminster	Usually £5 per transaction, but is at discretion of manager
Royal Bank of Scotland	No extra charge
TSB	Varies from region to region and is at discretion of manager

* In addition to stockbrokers commission.

If all this seems somewhat confusing the safest and fre-quently cheapest course is to stick to a stockbroker. A full list of member firms of the Stock Exchange is included on pages 124 to 158.

Defining your Needs

So how do you go about choosing a stockbroker? The best recommendation is obviously from a friend or associate. Failing that, the easiest starting point is to work out your own set of priorities. Do you want someone who can simply conclude small deals of around £300 for you? Do you want a broker who will give you regular advice? Do you need help with your tax returns and general investment as well as share tips?

If you simply plan to buy and sell a few small parcels of shares each year then you will probably do best with a small local dealer. Try three to start with. See how efficient they are in responding to your initial inquiry. Find out their minimum charges for small transactions. Cross check their ability to deal at the best prices for you.

In contrast, those looking for comprehensive advice, especially general investment planning, may be better off going to one of the larger city broking firms. The only caveat is that these City giants tend to recommend small clients, which by their definition covers those with less than £20,000 to invest in shares indirectly through unit trusts. However, there are signs that this attitude is shifting. In October 1986 stockbrokers will then offer a no-frills service to clients who they now consider too small to be profitable.

Buying on Credit

By the way, don't be upset if your stockbroker asks for references. Remember they will be carrying out your verbal instructions and effectively giving you a line of credit to buy shares. To understand how this works it is important to come to grips with the workings of the Stock Exchange and how the broker fits into the picture.

Just as Covent Garden used to be the market place for fruit and vegetables where retailers such as supermarkets and greengrocers shopped, so the floor of the Stock Exchange, in the heart of the City of London, is the hub of share activity. There are also four regional Stock Exchanges in Birmingham, Glasgow, Liverpool and Dublin, but now-adays they only transact a small percentage of overall securities business.

Although members of the public can view the activities of the exchange from a vantage point in the gallery above the trading floor they are not allowed to participate in the scene unfolding below. Imagine for a moment that you are looking down onto the trading floor. You will see a number of large booths manned predominantly by men who are known in the trade as jobbers. Jobbers are share wholesellers and they actually hold a stock of shares in various companies. Besides each jobber is a notice board with a list of prices at which he is prepared to buy and sell specific shares.

Wandering around the floor, stopping only to chat with jobbers at several booths will be the stockbrokers or their assistants. It is the stockbrokers task to buy or sell shares on behalf of his client and to conclude the deal on the most favourable terms. For their time and trouble they will earn a fee or commission based on the size of the transaction and the type of security purchased.

Each jobber sets his own price list. He is constantly changing the prices at which he is prepared to deal in line with any news about the company which might affect its share price or any flurry of buying or selling activity.

Setting Share Prices

Let's say a broker wishes to buy 1,000 Marks & Spencer shares for his client. He will ask the jobber for a quote or price on 1,000 Marks & Spencer shares. At this stage the jobber does not know whether the broker wishes to buy or sell M & S shares. He must quote two prices, the higher at which he is prepared to supply or sell M & S shares, which is known as the offer price, and a lower price, known as bid price, at which he is prepared to buy M & S shares. The difference between the two prices is known as the spread. In most cases the spread is around 2% for large actively dealt stocks but it may be considerably wider for shares in small companies or those where the price is moving sharply.

The broker will try several jobbers and then compare prices. Only when he decides to finalise the deal will he tell the jobber that in this case he is a buyer. The jobber cannot then go back on his word. The size of the transaction may be just a few hundred pounds or millions but the whole deal will be completed verbally.

The next step will be for the broker to report back to his client. The bill for the 1,000 M & S shares will only fall due at the end of what is called the account period. To simplify the workings of the exchange, the year is divided into 24 periods known as accounts. These usually run for two weeks and start on a Monday. Any transaction completed during the account does not have to be settled straight away. Instead there is a period of grace which can be up to three weeks if you buy at the start of the account. The final day of reckoning, known as settlement day, is ten days after the close of the account, i.e. normally the following Monday.

Chapter Seven
Clinching the Deal

Right. You've worked out what stocks or shares you wish to buy and have found a stockbroker or suitable person to arrange the transaction. Here are a few helpful hints to make sure your wishes are carried out to the letter.

Instructing your Broker

1. Always specify exactly how many shares you wish to buy. Brokers mentally think in thousands, so if you just rang up and asked to buy 500 ICI then he would purchase 500,000 ICI shares for you. The correct procedure is to ask him to buy 500 *shares* in ICI for you. Remember the same rule applies when it comes to selling.
2. Don't be vague about price. Before placing your buy or sell order, work out in your own mind the price range you are prepared to deal within. You can set limits for your broker by saying, for example, buy 500 shares in ICI at up to 600p, you can give him carte blanche and say buy 500 shares in ICI at best. Alternatively, you can ask him to check the current share price of ICI and order afterwards.

3. Ask your broker to 'report all bargains to you'. That way you'll know for certain that he has carried out your instructions and the price at which he dealt on your behalf.
4. If you go on holiday or are going to be out of touch you can leave your broker with a set of instructions in advance. You can give him specific buy or sell limits, by for example saying buy 500 shares in ICI at 200p and sell 500 shares in ICI at 650p.

Costs of the Transaction

When you buy stocks and shares, certain charges are fixed such as stamp duty, while other costs such as commission may vary depending upon whether you use a stockbroker, licensed dealer or bank.

Counting the Costs

1. Shares

Commission %	Band £
1.65	7,000
0.55	8,000
0.5	115,000
0.4	170,000

2. Debentures, Bonds & Convertibles

Commission %	Band £
0.9	5,000
0.45	5,000
0.35	40,000
0.325	80,000
0.25	770,000

3. Long Dated Gilts – over 10 years

Commission %	Band £
0.8	2,500
0.25	15,500
0.125	232,000

4. Medium Dated Gilts – 5 –10 years

Commission %	Band £
0.8	2,500
0.125	15,500
0.0625	232,000

At the moment stockbrokers have an agreement which regulates the amount of commission they charge on the purchase or sale of stated amounts of shares, debentures, bonds, convertibles, medium and long dated gilts. The table above indicates the amount of commission expressed as a percentage of the transaction. As you can see the system works on the principle that the more you buy the lower the percentage commission charged, but in order not to heavily penalise small investors, everyone has to pay the same rate on the smaller portions of their transaction. For example, if you buy £7,000 worth of shares you will pay brokers' commission at the rate of 1.65%. In contrast, if you buy £100,000 worth of shares you still pay 1.65% commission on the first £7,000, then 0.55% commission on the next £8,000 and 0.5% commission on the remaining £85,000. To show you the overall impact of this banding system we have calculated the commissions payable on transactions valued at £10,000, £20,000, £50,000 and £100,000.

Stockbrokers' Commission Charges in Pounds on Transactions of –

Category	£10,000	£20,000	£50,000	£100,000
Shares	£132.00	£184.50	£334.50	£584.50
Debentures, Bonds and Convertibles	£ 67.50	£102.50	£207.50	£370.00
Long dated Gilts	£ 38.75	£ 83.75	£121.25	£183.75
Medium dated Gilts	£ 29.37	£ 50.62	£ 69.37	£100.62

For small share transactions valued at less than £300, stockbrokers are free to set their own minimum charge. This varies from broker to broker and can be anything from £2 to £16. Generally speaking the larger City brokers are more expensive than the small regional ones. On short dated gilts, that is those due to mature in less than five years, most brokers usually charge the same rate as on medium dated gilt. VAT at 15% is payable on commissions.

Apart from commissions you have to pay 1% stamp duty on purchases which the broker collects on behalf of the government. No stamp duty is payable on sales so if you buy and sell a parcel of shares within an account you do not have to pay stamp duty. There is also a small charge for a contract stamp – normally 60p – and on large bargains over £5,000 a 60p levy to the Council for Securities Industry which monitors the workings of the exchange.

Total cost of buying £10,000 worth of shares through a stockbroker:–

Commission on £10,000	
1.65% on the first £7,000	£115.50
0.55% on the next £3,000	£ 15.00
Total commission	£130.50
VAT at 15% on the commission	£ 19.57
	£150.07
Stamp duty at 1% on £10,000	£100.00
Contract stamp	60
Grand Total	£250.67

Paperwork

Within 48 hours of buying or selling shares you should have received a contract note from your broker. This will give vital details of the transaction, name the share, the price at which it was bought or sold and specify the charges. It is essential you keep this contract note in a safe place as it is a legal record of the transaction and you may need to show it to the Inland Revenue at a later stage.

If you have just bought shares you will also receive a share certificate. The certificate is dispatched by the company or its registrars and may not arrive for several weeks. Don't worry, the contract note is proof that you own the shares.

When you come to sell, you need to dig out your share certificate and sign your name on a transfer form as renunciation. This should be posted back to your stockbroker so they can pass it on to the company registrar's who amend the records accordingly.

Chapter Eight
Common Situations Shareholders Face

As a shareholder you are entitled to receive regular information about the progress of the company in which you have chosen to invest. You will be asked to vote on all major changes of direction in the company's business, such as sizeable sales or purchases. For small investors this is very much a matter of rubber stamping the decisions taken by the management, often with the backing of major institutional shareholders such as pension funds and insurance companies. But in certain situations, such as take-overs or when a company is seeking to raise new money, the attitude of even relatively small shareholders can become crucial.

Scrip or Bonus Issue

When the share price of a company has risen very sharply its stockbrokers or financial advisers may suggest shareholders should be given a bonus or scrip issue. This is a method of increasing the number of shares issued and in theory should not effect the company's overall value.

For example, a company could have issued 10 million 25p

shares at 50p back in 1970. It's issued capital is 10 million × 25p which is £2.5m.

By 1985 the share price has risen dramatically and now stands at 500p. The price tag the stock market places on the company, known as its market capitalisation, is 10 million × 500p which is £50m.

Now the company makes a bonus issue of one share for every one held. It does this by issuing another 10 million 25p shares. The company's issued share capital doubles to 20 million × 25p which is £5m.

Existing shareholders will be sent renounceable share certificates giving them one new share for every share held. Shareholders in this situation do not need to pay any money. If you wish to keep the extra shares, simply detach the renounceable coupon from the bottom of the share certificate and place the certificate itself in a safe place.

What will be the effect of the bonus issue on the price of your existing shares? There will now be 20 million shares issued and the same amount of dividend to spread around. Earnings per share will have been halved. In theory the share price in this case should also halve to 250p, leaving the company's market value at £50m, i.e. 20 million shares × 250p.

In most cases, however, the company announces it plans to pay a maintained dividend on the new shares. In the above example, this would mean existing shareholders would receive twice as much in dividends. Such a decision combined with a growing company whose earnings are expanding fast would obviously support the price and probably result in an overall increase in the value of your shareholding.

Other than the effect on the share price, the result of the bonus or scrip issue is that the company's issued share capital more realistically reflects its underlying value. A bonus or share issue is a method fast growing companies frequently use to reward shareholders by distributing some of the company's past profits.

Splitting the Shares

For individual shareholders the result of a company deciding to split its shares is similar to the impact of a bonus issue.

The effect on a company's balance sheet is rather different. When a company makes a bonus issue it increases its issued share capital. When it splits it shares it is merely reducing the par or face value of its existing issued share capital and increasing the number of shares available.

Returning to our original example, the company has 10 million 25p shares in issue. It could decide to split each share into five shares with a par value of 5p. The company's issued share capital would then be 50 million × 5p which is £2.5 m.

As an existing shareholder, you will not be asked to pay any money for the additional shares. You will receive notification of the share split and should keep this attached to your original share certificate.

The effect of the share price should mirror the increase in the number of shares. In this case with each share being divided into five the price should fall to 100p. Again, any statement about dividends should be watched with care, although increased payouts are less common than with bonus issues.

In general shareholders tend to benefit from bonus issues and share splits as the price rarely falls sufficiently to compensate for the extra shares. If the company also announces a bigger overall dividend payout, there is a tangible gain. Remember to keep the new share certificates or any notice of share splits in a safe place as you may need the information for tax purposes at a later date.

Consolidation

The opposite procedure of a company splitting its shares is called consolidation. This is usually done when a company's share price has fallen and it often has a beneficial psychological impact on the share price.

Returning to our original example, let's assume the company has fallen on hard times, its share price has slumped from 100p when the shares were split in 1985 to 30p in 1990. The company decides to consolidate five 5p shares into one 25p share. This reduces the number of shares in issue. The issued share capital becomes 10 million × 25p which is £2.5 m.

In theory the share price should rise to reflect the decrease in the number of shares available. On a five to one consolidation the share price would increase five fold to 150p.

Existing shareholders need take no action. Simply keep details of the change alongside all your records of your holding in the company.

Capital Reconstruction

If a company runs into severe trouble, it will try to raise fresh money from whatever source it can manage. Sometimes the institutions or banks approached are only prepared to put in fresh money in return for substantial shareholdings in the company.

In such cases the holdings of existing shareholders are decreased to accommodate the needs of the new shareholders, without whose money the business would grind to a halt and be worthless. Usually a complex package of capital reconstruction is developed and existing ordinary shareholders may find their ordinary shares are swopped for newly issued shares or loan stock which rank behind the shares held by the institutions which are bailing out the company.

Existing shareholders should usually grit their teeth and accept the package offered. Often this is a last ditch attempt to save a company and if shareholders vote against the proposal their holdings are likely to be worthless anyway.

Rights Issues

When a company wants to raise new money either for a special venture or simply to expand its existing business it often approaches its existing shareholders and gives them first refusal. The process is known as a rights issue because existing shareholders have the right to buy a fixed number of shares directly related to their holding at a stated price.

It is vital that you read the document describing the rights issue, its price and purpose with care. If you need advice don't hesitate to consult your broker or financial adviser.

Let's go back to the company we originally described. It has 10 million 25p shares now standing at 500p in the market. The company wishes to buy out one of its small competitors for £8m. Its financial advisers suggest a one for five rights issue at 400p. That means for every five shares in the company you hold you will be offered the chance to buy another one share at the fixed price of 400p.

From the company's point of view it will be issuing two million new 25p shares at 400p which increases its issued share capital to $12m \times 25p$ which is £3m and will raise $2m \times 400p$ which is £8m.

Let's assume you hold 5,000 shares with a current market value of £25,000. You will be offered 1,000 new shares at 400p which will cost you £4,000. To see whether this represents good value add the current market price of five shares, i.e. $5 \times 500p$ which is £25 to the value of one new share which is £4, i.e. £29 and divide by 6, the total number of shares, the answer is 483p. The difference between this figure of 483p and the rights issue price of 400p represents the premium built into the rights. In theory once the new shares have been issued all the shares would be trading in the market at 483p.

As an existing shareholder you will be sent a provisional renounceable allotment letter for 1,000 new shares at 400p. You must now decide what you wish to do:–

1. Take up all the new shares offered

If you think the company's prospects are sound, you can afford to buy the new shares and you do not wish to reduce your overall percentage holding in the company, then you can take up your rights. You do this by returning the provisional allotment letter together with a cheque for the new shares, in this case £4,000, to the address stated in the document. In due course you will receive a share certificate for the new holding.

2. Take up some of the rights offered

If you cannot afford to buy all the new shares or only wish to invest a bit more money in this company then it is possible to take up some of the new shares offered and sell the rest. First you sign the renunciation form on the back of the allotment letter. Then send the letter with your instructions to your broker who will complete the deal on your behalf.

3. Sell the rights

If you do not wish to invest further in the company then you can sell your rights to the new shares. There is a market in allotment letters and your broker will arrange the sale for you. Once again you must renounce the letter. The price you will receive will be the difference between the adjusted share price of all the shares and the rights price. In this case 483p – 400p, minus a small amount to reflect the buying costs. So on 1,000 shares you could expect to make about 80p × 1,000 which is £800.

As you can see it is essential that you take some action. If you do nothing you are missing your best opportunity to make a profit. However, the company itself will sell at a net premium all rights which have not been taken up by the payment date and send you the net proceeds.

You should watch the movements in the share price of the old shares closely. If the company is highly regarded and it is expected to produce substantially higher earnings on the new money, then the share price may not fall back as much as theory dictates. Conversely if the company is making a last ditch attempt to raise money and no one else wishes to invest further, its share price might fall more steeply and in the most severe conditions the rights may be worthless.

So much for existing investors in a company. If you wish to buy shares in a company for the first time, buying the rights is often a relatively cheap way of going about it. There is no commission and no stamp duty on the purchase and the price is usually pitched very attractively, but you should remember it is a cash purchase.

Chapter Nine
Takeovers

If you hold shares in a company which is subject to takeover then you are likely to make a handsome profit. The bidding company will normally offer to buy your shares at a price above the market value before the bid was announced. The bid may consist of cash, the bidder's shares or a mixture of the two.

Rules of the Game

There are strict rules governing the conduct and action of both parties during a takeover. The Takeover Panel, a self-regulatory body, keeps a meticulous eye on the statements and behaviour of both predator and bid victims. The Panel aims to ensure that all shareholders are treated equally and that no wildly unsubstantiated or misleading statements are made in the heat of the takeover battle.

Under existing rules, once a company owns more than 29.9% of a quoted company it is required to make a full bid for the rest of the shares. If it holds no shares in the target company it may set the price of its offer at whatever level it thinks will win support. However, if the bidder has purchased shares in the market giving it 15% or more of the target company then it cannot offer existing shareholders less than the highest price it has paid within the last 12 months and the offer must either be in cash or provide a cash alternative.

There are basically three types of bids: agreed, contested and rescue. The action of shareholders in the target company should vary depending upon the type of bid and prospects of its success.

Agreed Bid

A bid is said to be agreed if it has the support of the target company's directors. Providing the management hold a majority stake in the company then the bid has an above average chance of success. Existing shareholders have little choice but to accept the offer at the last possible moment, unless a higher bidder can convince the controlling shareholders of the merit of their offer.

However, if the directors do not hold a majority stake then there is still all to play for and the outcome is by no means certain.

Contested Bid

This is the most common situation. As a shareholder you will be inundated with documents purporting to establish the superiority of both contestants. The outcome in these cases is also uncertain.

Rescue Bid

When a company gets into trouble and seeks outside assistance, it may turn not to a bank or financial institution but to another company for help. The rescuer will take a stake in the ailing company in return for giving its assistance. In such cases even though the rescuer may acquire more than 29.9% in the sick company it can be relieved by the Takeover Panel from bidding for the remaining shares.

When you receive details of the takeover offer first find out what type of bid you are facing. If it is an agreed bid with support from the directors with more than 50% of the shares, you should accept the offer. Where there is an alternative between cash and shares, remember that if you opt for cash this counts as a sale of your holdings for tax purposes. If you merely swop shares in the target company for those in the bidder you are not deemed to have sold your shares as far as the taxman is concerned. Apart from tax considerations, you should obviously consider the future prospects of the bidding company before accepting shares in the merged group.

If the offer is a rescue, then you can do nothing but be grateful an outside company is prepared to inject cash into a sick business. Such action may support the share price of the ailing company and improve its long term chances of recovery.

Finally, if the bid is contested or it is backed by a management which does not have a majority shareholding, then you must analyse the terms carefully, watch the market price of the share and assess the prospects for the bid's success.

When a bid is announced, the share price of the target company usually rises. If the market thinks the bid will succeed the share price will increase until it equals the price offered by the bidder. However, sometimes the share price stays well below the bid price which indicates the market view that the bid will fail. Finally, sometimes the share price rises above the bid which in turn means the market either expects a higher offer from the same bidder or another better bid from a third party.

As a shareholder, you must weigh up the possibility of the bid's success. As a general rule it pays to wait until the last moment so you can see whether a higher offer is forthcoming. However, do check the terms carefully. Sometimes the cash alternative is only available for a limited period. You will only receive the price stated in the offer if the bid is successful, so if you are in any doubt, you may wish to make a profit by selling your shares in the market before the offer expires.

Once a bidder receives acceptances from more than 50% of the shareholders the offer goes unconditional and at that stage you will be holding shares in a subsidiary of the bidder. If the bidder has acceptances of 90% then it can compulsorily acquire the outstanding shares under the conditions of the offer on application to the courts.

If the bid fails and the would-be purchaser cannot obtain support from more than half the shareholders, then the offer lapses. The bidder is left with any shares it bought in the market and cannot make another bid for a year. Any acceptances which have been delivered will be returned.

Chapter Ten
Getting in at the Ground Floor

The first chance the general public has to invest in most companies is when they issue shares which are traded on one of the established share markets, either The Stock Exchange itself, the Unlisted Securities Market or the Over-the-Counter Market. Not surprisingly the term given to these freshly minted shares is a new issue.

Cashing In

Why do companies sell their shares to the public? The simple answer is to raise cash. A private company has limited access to finance. It can turn to its bank for a loan at the going rate of interest or try to raise further capital from its existing limited band of shareholders. By making a new issue and selling shares to the general public a company has turned the tap on a huge potential cash flow. It also gives the founder shareholders an opportunity of selling part of their holdings.

The other chief reason for a new issue is political. The Thatcher government has a stated policy of privatising major sections of industry currently owned by the state.

Privatisation has become something of a vogue word in recent years. It simply consists of the government selling shares in a nationalised industry to the public. The largest such exercise to date was the sale of 50.2% of British Telecom in November 1984 which netted the government £1.352 bn.

Privatisation Schedule

Date	Company	£m Net Proceeds
1978–79	British Petroleum	276
1978–79	British Technology Group et al	94
1980–81	British Aerospace	43
1980–81	British Technology Group et al	167
1981–82	British Petroleum	8
1981–82	British Sugar Corporation	44
1981–82	Cable and Wireless	182
1981–82	Amersham International	64
1981–82	National Freight Company	5
1981–82	British Technology Group et al	191
1982–83	Britoil	334
1982–83	Associated British Ports	46
1982–83	International Aeradio [1]	60
1982–83	British Rail Hotels [1]	30
1982–83	British Technology Group et al	75
1983–84	British Petroleum	543
1983–84	Cable and Wireless	263
1983–84	Britoil	293
1983–84	British Rail Hotels	15
1983–84	British Technology Group et al	43
1984–85	Associated British Ports [2]	51
1984–85	British Gas Corporation Onshore Oil Assets [1]	82
1984–85	Enterprise Oil	380
1984–85	Sealink [1]	40
1984–85	Jaguar [1]	297
1984–85	British Telecom (first instalment)	1,352
1984–85	British Technology Group et al	208

1985 – 86	British Aerospace[3]	346
1985 – 86	Sealink[1]	26
1985 – 86	British Telecom[4] (second instalment)	1,160

[1] Proceeds retained by parent company.
[2] Estimates to date.
[3] Some costs not finalised. Final instalment due in April 1986.
[4] Some costs not yet finalised. Second instalment due in September 1986.

Source: The Treasury

There are four more new issues planned by the government. These are:–
- British Airways.
- British Shipbuilders Warshipbuilding Yards.
- Royal Ordnance plc.
- National Bus Company.

In addition, the government has announced it will introduce legislation:–
- To enable the privatisation of British Gas Corporation and the British Airports Authority.

During the lifetime of the present parliament the government also hopes to privatise:–
- Parts of British Steel and British Leyland.
- Rolls Royce.
- Short Brothers.

The government is also looking at the possibility of a measure of privatisation in the water industry as well as trying to attract private capital into the electricity industry.

How it's Done

When a company wants to issue shares it will first approach a bank or stockbroker who specialises in handling all the arrangements. This institution is known as the issuing house and they are responsible for masterminding the whole operation from start to finish. Before a company can sell shares to the public it must prepare a legal document known as a prospectus giving full and accurate information about its trading history, track record and management. It is the responsibility of the directors to ensure that the details given in the prospectus are true and correct. It is on the basis of this document that investors will decide whether to buy shares in the company.

There are three ways of selling new shares to the public: –

1. An offer for sale at a fixed price. The company and the issuing house together set the price at which they are prepared to sell the shares.

2. Offer for sale by tender. The company and its advisers establish a minimum selling price and potential shareholders have to name their own price. The highest offers are satisfied.

3. Placing. This is the sale of the shares at a fixed price to an agreed list of investors, usually institutions such as stockbrokers or insurance companies.

It is not always easy for individual investors to keep track of new issues. If the shares are subsequently to be fully listed then copies of the full prospectus must appear in two national dailies. However, if the shares are to be traded on the Unlisted Securities Market only a box advertisement giving bare details is required. For marketing reasons most companies coming to the USM will publish a full prospectus. Details of over-the-counter new issues are likely only to be available direct from the issuing house.

Buying and Selling

Once you have found about a new issue and have decided you wish to invest, what happens next?

1. Offer for sale at a fixed price. Simply fill in the application form at the back of the prospectus or from the newspaper clipping stating the number of shares you wish to buy and enclosing a cheque for the total cost. Make sure you send it to the stated address and allow plenty of time for hold-ups in the post. Applications received after the specified deadline will not be considered.

2. Offer for sale by tender. This is a rather more complex transaction and it is probably best to seek financial

advice. You don't want to pay over the odds for the shares nor do you want to miss out on the opportunity to invest by pitching your price too low. Once you have decided on the price you are prepared to pay fill in the form and follow the postal instructions.

In both cases it is important that you use the actual form included in the prospectus. Photocopies do not count. Also be careful to state your name and address clearly and correctly.

3. Placing. It is extremely unlikely that individual investors will be offered shares in a placing direct but they may be offered shares from a placing via their stockbroker. Here it is simply a matter of a verbal instruction to your broker if you wish to buy some shares in the new issue.

After you have filled the relevant forms in correctly and posted them in good time to meet the deadline, what happens next? It's nail biting time. The merchant bank or broker who is acting as the issuing house will spend the next few days opening letters and trying to assess the overall demand. A statement may be given to the press indicating the number of applications that have been received.

Then the issuing house will sort out the applications in greater detail and having analysed the response work out a formula for allocating the shares. For example, some investors may be satisfied in full and others could find their name going into a ballot. Multiple applications may be weeded out. If the sale is by tender the maths is rather more complicated with the issuing house having to balance the size of an application and the price.

If it is a large issue, particularly a privatisation, the first news you will get of the likely success of your application will be from the newspapers. They will detail the basis of allocation. It may be several days later before you actually receive confirmation that you have been allotted shares. Don't be misled by the fact that your cheque has been cashed. This does not necessarily mean your application has been granted in full. With prompt service on the part of the issuing house and the post office you should know for certain before dealings start.

If you are successful in applying for shares you will find

a letter of allotment in the post. This will tell you how many shares you now own. You have three choices, to keep all the shares, to sell part of your holding or to sell all the shares. Let's assume you decide to keep the shares. You can simply file away the letter of allotment and wait for the share certificate to arrive from the company. Alternatively you can speed up the procedure by sending the letter of allotment to the company's registrars who will in turn forward your share certificate. It's best to keep a photocopy of the original allotment for your records and for tax purposes. So much for the long term investor. Many people sell shares in new issues straight away in the hope of making a quick profit. They are called stags. If you wish to sell some or all of the shares simply sign the renunciation form on the back of the allotment letter and your broker will arrange the sale on your behalf. Your broker will send you a contract note detailing the sale which should be kept safely and if you still hold shares the certificate of ownership will arrive in due course from the company's registrars. There is no commission or stamp duty payable on the sale of allotment letters.

Pros and Cons

New issues are usually priced very attractively and the share price is pitched at the level the issuing house thinks will generate enough buyers to take up all the shares available. However, there is many a slip between fixing the price and the first day's dealings. For a start there could be a gap of up to two weeks. A few days is a long time in stock market terms and sentiment about an issue can swing violently.

So don't be misled by reports of quick killings by investors selling new issues on the first day of dealings. Before sending off your cheque consider the following questions:–

a) What direction are prices in the market likely to be moving? If share prices are rising steadily, go onto the next question. If not, it's probably best to sit this one out.

b) Is it a company I would be happy to hold shares in at the offer price regardless of what happens in the first flurry of dealings? If your answer is no. What makes you think other people will buy the shares from you at a higher price? Unless you can come up with a good reason, stop right here. If you can honestly, answer yes, then go ahead and apply for the shares.

How Government Privatisation Issues have Fared

Company	Issue Price	Issue Date	Price on 16/8/1985	Change %
British Aerospace	375p	May 1985	355p	− 5.3
Cable and Wireless	275p	Dec 1983	530p	+ 92.7
Amersham	142p	Feb 1982	330p	+ 132.4
Associated British Ports	270p	Apr 1984	288p	+ 6.6p
Enterprise Oil	185p	Jun 1984	180p	− 2.7
Jaguar	165p	July 1984	426p	+ 158.2
British Telecom	90p*	Nov 1984	195p	+ 116.6

*Adjusted for second instalment.

On the whole private investors have made substantial profits if they were lucky enough to be allotted shares in government privatisation issues. The exception was Britoil when 51% of the oil exploration company's shares were sold for 215p in November 1982 and never managed to reach this price level again. When the government sold its second chunk of shares in Britoil the market's view was reflected in the offer price of 185p in August 1985.

If you are not allotted shares but believe the company is worth investing in, it may be worth buying shares on the first day of dealings. Anyone who had done this in the case of British Telecom could have doubled their money in six months.

Chapter Eleven
Getting in at the Basement

The earliest opportunity the general public normally has of buying shares in a company is when these are quoted for the first time on the stock market or traded on the Unlisted Securities Market or Over-the-Counter market. By this stage the company may well have passed the crucial make or break period and although its future success is not assured the odds on it staying the course have increased considerably.

Business Expansion Scheme

To encourage investors to back new ventures at an earlier stage the Thatcher government introduced the Business Expansion Scheme in 1983. The aim is to compensate for the high risks involved in locking your money away in growing unquoted companies by giving income tax relief at the highest level on investments of up to £40,000 per year. The scheme is obviously more attractive to higher rate taxpayers than standard rate taxpayers as the table opposite indicates.

Tax Rate	Gross Investment	Net Investment
30%	£40,000	£28,000
45%	£40,000	£22,000
50%	£40,000	£20,000
60%	£40,000	£16,000

There are strict rules about which companies qualify for the Business Expansion Scheme and the investment must be held for five years.

The chief requirements are that:–

- The company is trading wholly or mainly in the UK.
- It is seeking new risk capital for genuine additional investments.
- The capital must come from outside investors.
- The company must be involved in a risk activity.

Since the scheme was first introduced in 1983 the government has gradually refined the regulations in an attempt to exclude lower risk companies such as those involving property and agricultural land. The current scheme runs until April 1987.

Choosing a Company

It cannot be stressed too often that companies qualifying for the Business Expansion Scheme are by their very nature high risk. Even if the company itself prospers you may find it difficult to sell your holdings for a fair price after five years has elapsed. However, it is possible to reduce some of the risks by spreading your investments between various companies, taking full advantage of professional advice and reading the small print carefully.

The first task is to see whether the company itself represents an interesting investment opportunity. Check:–

1. What does the company do? Is this a high risk industry with a poor record for new small companies or an area where small firms traditionally do well?
2. How experienced are the directors? Are you backing men and women with proven management and financial expertise or newcomers to the business? Is there sufficient depth of financial advice at board level to ensure any

expansion does not overstretch the company's balance sheet?

3. What, if any, information is available about the company's trading record? Are there any indications about future performance such as firm orders?
4. What assets does the company have? Does the company hold any freeholds or leaseholds? What is its stock position? Is this stock saleable?
5. What do the directors plan to do with the money? Are they developing new products? Marketing existing services? Going into export?
6. Are they raising sufficient cash for their purposes?
7. What is the standing of the companies outside professional advisers?
8. Is there any indication of whether the company plans to have its shares traded on a recognised market in the foreseeable future?

Terms of the Issue
The next step is to see whether the terms on which you are being offered the shares are attractive. Check:–

1. What percentage of the company's shares are available?
2. What holdings do the directors have now?
3. What rights or options do the directors or their advisers have to buy shares in the future?
4. What fees are being charged for the issue?
5. What percentage of your money will actually be invested in the company?
6. How much money will the directors be taking out of the business in terms of salaries and bonuses?
7. How much will the outside financial advisers be paid?

The answers to these questions should help you decide whether you are being offered a fair crack of the whip. In particular pay attention to the fees and the right of directors to buy shares at a future date on relatively cheap terms.

The Fund Route
If choosing which companies to invest in seems too onerous then you can delegate the process to a fund manager. Of course you will end up paying the fund manager a fee to

cover their expertise and work in hand picking the investments.

Most of the funds are structured as unauthorised unit trusts. That means they sell investors units in a pooled fund. As the trust is unauthorised there are no rules laid down on how the units are priced or the arrangements to be made for unit holders seeking their money back. However, the Department of Trade does insist that full details on these and other critical points are included in the fund prospectus.

It also lays down some minimum requirements. These include: –

- No more than 25% of the initial funds available will be invested in a single company.
- No money will be invested in a company where the manager has a material interest.
- Interest in the company's shares will be allocated pro rata to subscriptions.
- Regular reports at intervals of not more than six months will be sent to investors.
- No money must be invested until the last subscription date has passed.
- Investors money should be paid into a separate trust account during the subscription period.

There is considerable flexibility on how these funds are structured so potential investors should pay particular attention to the small print. Many recent funds for example state that investors cannot obtain their money back until five years has elapsed. The subsequent arrangements for cashing individual holdings should also be scrutinised with care to ensure that fair treatment is received both by investors wishing to withdraw their money and those who choose to remain as unitholders. Since the underlying shares are not quoted you must also examine the system which will be adopted when calculating the value of the holdings.

Other points to check: –

- Arrangements for any dividend payments.
- Arrangements for spare cash from sale of investments.
- Extent of managers powers in selecting investments and exercising voting rights.

- Ceiling for investment in one company.
- Managers fee.
- Charges.
- Any special arrangements involving the managers purchase of shares in companies the fund has invested in.

The Future

There are plans at the moment for some of the institutions most active in this area to set up a market in BES company shares. This would make it easier for direct investors to sell their holdings in Business Expansion Scheme companies, for the companies themselves to raise cash and also, of course, leave open the possibility of take-overs. In addition, if fund managers knew there was at least a limited market for BES company shares then they could be more flexible in their attitude towards individual investors wanting to withdraw their cash before five years had elapsed.

Chapter Twelve
Investing Overseas

There are no restrictions on moving your money around the world. Since the Thatcher government abolished exchange controls in 1979 British investors have been free to take their pick of the international stock markets. Although the City of London is one of the world's largest and most sophisticated financial centres there may be times when you wish to buy shares in foreign companies quoted on overseas stock markets.

Currency Considerations

When you buy shares overseas there is an extra dimension involved. Of course it is essential to make sure the company you have chosen is a solid investment in its own right but it is equally vital to take a view on the currency risk. To show you how the two factors work in concert, consider the four examples below.

a) The share price rises and sterling strengthens against the dollar. You invest £1,000 in American shares when the pound stands at $1.20. This gives you a portfolio worth $1,200. Six months later the price of your shares has risen by 10% valuing your holding at $1,320. Sterling has strengthened against the dollar and now stands at $1.50. You sell your shares and convert the proceeds into sterling. You receive £880 – that's a 12% loss.

b) The share price rises and sterling weakens against the dollar. You invest £1,000 in American shares when the pound stands at $1.20. This gives you a portfolio worth $1,200. Six months later the price of your shares has risen by 10% valuing your holding at $1,320. Sterling has weakened against the dollar and now stands at $1. You sell your shares and convert the proceeds into sterling. You pocket £1,320 – that's a 32% profit.

c) The share price falls and sterling strengthens against the dollar. You invest £1,000 in American shares when the pound stands at $1.20. This gives you a portfolio worth $1,200. Six months later the price of your shares has fallen by 10% valuing your holding at $1,080. Sterling has strengthened against the dollar and now stands at $1.50. You sell your shares and convert the proceeds into sterling. You end up with £720 – that's a 28% loss.

d) The share price falls and sterling weakens against the dollar. You invest £1,000 in American shares when the pound stands at $1.20. This gives you a portfolio worth $1,200. Six months later the price of your shares has fallen by 10% valuing your holdings at $1,080. Sterling has weakened against the dollar and now stands at $1. You sell your shares and convert the proceeds into sterling. You net £1,080 – that's an 8% profit.

The table shows how share prices have moved over the last ten years in 11 major financial markets. Column A shows the average annual return in local currency and Column B translates these gains into sterling. Over the period 1975-84 sterling's weakness against the major world currencies helped boost the return for UK investors overseas. But a very different pattern has started to emerge in 1985 with sterling's strength reducing the value of overseas investments.

So if the message is, if sterling is strengthening against, say, the dollar, then you will need less and less pounds to buy each dollar and conversely your dollar holdings will be worth less in sterling. If sterling is weakening against the

How Currency effects the
Return on International Equities

% per annum	COLUMN A Annual returns in local currencies Average 75–84	COLUMN B Annual returns in sterling 75–84*
USA	14.8	23
Japan	14.8	25
United Kingdom	31.7	32
Canada	15.4	20
Germany	12.5	16**
Australia	18.1	21
Switzerland	10.0	18
France	19.4	19
Singapore	17.9	27
Netherlands	22.2	27
Hong Kong	26.6	30

* Figures have been rounded up
** Excluding German tax credit   Source: Phillips & Drew

dollar, you will need more and more pounds to buy each dollar but your dollar holdings will be worth an increasing number of pounds. In an ideal world you would buy foreign shares when sterling was at its strongest and sell when the pound was at its weakest.

Check List

Before buying foreign shares, ask your broker the following questions: –

1. *What types of stock are available?*
   In the UK, shares are registered. That means each shareholder receives a share certificate from the company itself and his or her name is placed on the share register. Even if you lose your share certificate there is still an independent and valid record that the shares are in fact

owned by you. In many foreign markets, particularly the USA, the stock is in what is called bearer form. There is no central registration and the stock belongs to whoever physically holds it.

2. *What is the minimum size in which I can deal?*
For investors in the UK who are used to buying shares which are quoted in pennies and rarely cost more than a couple of pounds each, it is difficult to adjust to foreign prices where shares can cost hundreds of pounds each. The exact cost of each share can be vital in markets such as Tokyo where the minimum order is 1,000 shares.

3. *What arrangements will be made for delivery of stock?*
Most brokers are keen to dissuade their clients from taking personal delivery of the stock. They argue it is time consuming and makes quick sales inflexible. Provided your broker is reputable and you are satisfied the arrangements are secure then it may be less hassle to allow him to store the shares overseas for you. Make sure the documentation is in order and that the charges are reasonable. A handling charge per annum of between £10 and £15 is par for the course and for an additional fee you should also receive your dividends paid direct in pounds.

4. *Will my dividends be paid in sterling or foreign currency?*
Most companies naturally enough pay dividends only in their own currency. However, a number of large American companies who are keen to encourage foreign investors pay dividends in sterling. This can save you time, trouble and money. In the past, many shareholders who asked their bank to change small dividend cheques into sterling found the fees involved were higher than the size of the dividend payout.

5. *How much will the transaction cost?*
If you go through your normal broker you are likely to end up paying his fee plus the commission charged by the local broker. Unless you plan to buy sizeable amounts of foreign shares you will just have to grin and bear this. Commissions around the world vary considerably. In the

USA, for example, there are no set fees and it is possible to buy shares quite cheaply from a so-called share boutique. To give you an idea of comparative costs we asked one of the country's largest brokers, Quilter Goodison, how much they would charge a client buying £10,000 worth of shares in Frankfurt, Hong Kong, New York and Tokyo. They charge £280.55 on bargains of £10,000 in Hong Kong, Germany and Tokyo and £180.55 in New York where there is no stamp duty. If you wish them to look after the stock for you they will charge £10 a year plus £5 per dividend payment. That can add up to a further £30 per year on a US stock which pays dividends quarterly. If you plan to invest regularly in a particular foreign market you should make contact with a foreign broker based in the UK.

6. *Will you keep me up-to-date with advice and information about my investment?*
As a shareholder you will receive the company's report and accounts and any special statements. However, this may be of limited use if it arrives in Japanese, six weeks later. So it is important to try and secure a more efficient source of information. Ideally you should choose a broker with an office in the country where you plan to invest and one which provides regular research on shares in your chosen market.

Foreign Stocks Quoted in London

Many of the world's largest companies have their shares quoted in London. This makes it much easier for UK investors to buy their shares. Your broker should be able to tell you whether a share you are considering is available in London.

There are now 505 overseas companies with London quotes. The majority are American but there is also a sizeable number of South African gold and mining shares included.

Chapter Thirteen
The Fixed Rate Option

Shares offer the chance of making substantial profits. They also involve accepting a certain level of risk and short term price fluctuation. If you want to play rather safe then you should consider choosing an investment which pays a stated rate of interest and is repaid at face value on a specified date.

Calculating the Return

While it is impossible to predict the return on an investment in shares it is easy to work out the sums on a fixed rate investment provided you hold the stock until it is repaid or redeemed. The most essential feature to grasp is the difference between the flat yield and the redemption yield. Both are quoted gross, that is without deduction of tax. The flat yield reflects the amount of interest you receive in a year expressed as a percentage of the price you paid for the stock. For example, say you bought stock 2000 10% at £100. Then for every £100 you would receive £10 each year giving a flat yield of 10% gross. In contrast, say you bought stock 2000 10% at £90 then your flat yield would be 10/90 which is 11.1% gross. If you bought the same stock at £120 then your flat yield would be 10/120 which is 8.3% gross. So you can see when the price of the stock rises the yield falls and when the price falls the yield rises.

The yield to redemption is based on the return you would receive if you held the stock until it was repaid at face value or par. That means if you bought stock at £100 and it was repaid at £100 the flat yield and the yield to redemption would be the same. But let's go back and take a look at the other two cases. We will assume it is year 1990 and you are considering buying stock 2000 10% which is standing at £90. For every £90 invested you will receive £10 in income each year and in the year 2000 you will be repaid £100. The yield to redemption consists of the interest you receive each year, i.e. £10, plus your capital gain worked out on an annual basis. In this case you make a £10 capital gain over ten years which on an annual basis is £1. This is added to the £10 in interest you receive each year making a total of £11. The redemption yield is £11 divided by £90 or 12.2% gross.

Let's compare this with the second case. The stock is standing at £120. You still receive your £10 in interest each year but this time you will be sitting on capital loss of £120 – £100, i.e. £20. Over ten years this is equivalent to a loss of £2 per year. You deduct this from the interest received each year £10 – £2 = £8. The redemption yield is £8 divided by £120 or 6.6% gross.

So you see how important it is to work out the redemption yield and compare this with the flat yield. Luckily you don't have to do all the sums yourself each time as most national papers will quote both yields but it is important to grasp the distinction when deciding how to invest.

Stock Picking

There is a huge range of fixed rate investments for you to choose. You can lend money to foreign governments, international agencies, the UK government, local authorities and companies. Generally the more prestigious the borrower the less they will be prepared to pay for your money. In other words, you have to decide for yourself the trade off you are willing to make between the return and the risk.

On the whole it is best to stick to loans in sterling to the UK government, known as gilts or those to international agencies, local authorities or major companies.

Tax
Before deciding which stock to buy you should check up on the tax position. You will have to pay income tax at your current level on all interest received. If you sell the stock for more than you paid you may be liable to capital gains tax. There is no capital gains tax on gilts held over a year but there is on the rest. However, since you can make tax free capital gains of up to £5,900 in the year 1985-86 this is unlikely to bite where small investors are concerned.

When to Buy Fixed Rate Stocks
As a general rule of thumb you should aim to buy fixed rate stocks just as interest rates start to fall. That way you lock into high rates of annual income and the price of the stock itself will start to rise, pushing down the yield for new investors into line with the rest of the economy. This gives you a potential capital gain as well as the security of high income.

Unfortunately, life is not quite so simple and it is not always easy to say when rates are going to move up or down. If you get your timing wrong, it will not effect your return if you hold the stock until it is repaid. However, if rates start to rise then the price of the stock will fall until the yield is in line with the rest of the economy.

So, before deciding to buy gilts, ask yourself two things: Do I want income or growth? What is my time scale?

a) **Maximum Income**
   Go for stock with highest gross yields maturing at a distant date.

b) **Capital**
   Go for stock with highest redemption yield which is standing below face value.

c) **Short term capital gain**
   Only invest if you think interest rates are falling. Go for highest flat yield.

Don't buy if:

a) Interest rates are rising.

b) Inflation is likely to be higher than the rates of return offered on gilts.

Inflation Factor

When you invest in a fixed rate investment you know in money terms exactly what interest you will receive and how much you will be repaid on redemption. What you cannot know in advance is how much those pounds will be worth in terms of spending power. This depends upon the level of inflation. While a return of 12% may look very attractive when inflation is running at around 6%, it would look pretty miserable if inflation took off to say 20%. If that happened your savings would actually shrink.

To provide investors who are worried about inflation with an option to protect the real value of their money, the Thatcher government introduced index-linked gilts in 1982. These guarantee to repay investors the face value of the stock fully adjusted for inflation. They tend to have low flat yields and when you wish to calculate the redemption yield you have to do so by making an assumption about the level of inflation. Again, most papers will provide data based on two calculations, allowing for different levels of inflation and your financial adviser will do the sums for you at whatever rate you think is appropriate.

Since their introduction, index-linked gilts have been out performed by traditional gilts. That's because index-linked gilts tend to be bought for capital appreciation rather than income, while ordinary gilts pay interest in line with the rest of the economy. With inflation pushed down to single figures and interest rates falling, demand for index-linked gilts has been a trickle while ordinary gilts have proved attractive to both income and capital seekers. As interest rates have declined, prices have risen throwing up capital gains and with inflation several points beneath the yield on gilts investors wanting income are currently obtaining a real return on their money.

Risk versus Return

If you are new to the investment world it is probably wisest to concentrate on gilts. However, if you wish to be a bit more adventurous and earn on average about 1% more on your money you could consider what are called bulldogs. These are sterling loans to international borrowers. Prices tend to be reasonably stable and move parallel to gilts unless some crisis blows up. For this reason stick to bulldogs issued by international agencies and Western Europe countries with stable governments.

More risky and with an even higher return are loan stocks issued by companies. Here it is a matter of making sure you are happy with an investment in this particular company and not simply being lured by the interest rate.

Sources of Information

The Stock Exchange Official List will give details of gilts, bulldogs and company loan stocks. Most papers quote daily prices and yields of gilts but do not have a comprehensive coverage of loan stocks issued by companies. Many stockbrokers produce booklets for their clients summarising the stocks available and quoting recent prices. You should be able to obtain one of these free of charge from your broker.

Where to Buy

You can buy all the stocks mentioned here through your broker. About half the gilts on sale can also be purchased from your local post office. The number of gilts on the list is being constantly increased and if you cannot find the gilt you wish to buy below then check with your post office. An up-to-date leaflet is available from Bonds & Stock Office, Blackpool, Lancashire FY3 9YP. Telephone: 0253-697333 (anytime).

If you are buying less than £1,000 worth of gilts it is cheaper to go to the post office, but for larger deals your broker is better value. Cost aside, the chief consideration should be whether you wish to receive your interest gross, without tax deducted, or net of standard rate tax. Gilts bought from the post office pay interest gross while those bought via your broker pay net of standard rate tax.

Chapter Fourteen
A Matter of Tax

The final piece in the investment jigsaw is tax. Many people are tempted into high risk schemes simply on the grounds these minimise tax. This can be a great mistake. Far better to pay the taxman a portion of your gains than to end up with huge losses – even if these can be set against your tax bill.

Capital Gains

For investors who have previously left their money in building societies, banks or national savings the main distinction to grasp is the difference between income and capital gains. Any money you receive while you hold your investment, such as dividends on shares or interest on loan stock, is treated as income and subject to tax at your income tax rate. The difference between the buying and selling price of stocks and shares is a capital gain or loss. If these gains do not exceed the annual exemption set each year then you do not have to pay capital gains tax. If the gains exceed the exemption then you pay tax on that amount over and above your annual exemption at the rate of 30%. So for the year 1985-86 the capital gains annual exemption is £5,900. Provided your gains fall short of this sum there is no tax bill. If say, you made gains of £6,900 then you would pay capital gains tax on £6,900 – £5,900 which is £1,000 at 30%, giving a tax bill of £300.

Indexation

In the 1982 Budget the government introduced the concept of indexation of capital gains. The idea was that investors should not have to pay tax on gains which simply matched the rise in the retail prices index. So for example if a share had risen by 10% over a period when inflation had risen by 10% there was no real gain and therefore no potential tax liability.

Simple as the idea sounds in principle, working out the nitty gritty calculations turned out to be extremely complex. So in the 1985 Budget the government introduced new rules to make it easier to calculate your capital gains tax bill. It also extended the concept of indexation to losses which has restored the symmetry of the tax burden.

Doing the Sums

To work out your tax bill you need three figures:–
1. The cost of the shares including brokerage and stamp duty.
2. The price you sold the shares at, less any brokerage.
3. The rise in the retail prices index over the relevant period.

Let's start with 1. Simple enough you might think. You dig out your contract notes for the shares, look at the total cost paid to your broker and make a note of this sum. This is your acquisition cost.

If, however, your shares were purchased before 6 April 1982 then the indexation allowance can be calculated either on the original cost or the value of the shares on 31st March 1982, provided you owned them at that date. In order to maximise your indexation allowance you should opt for the higher of the two prizes. Your stockbroker or financial adviser should be able to give you the appropriate prices of shares as at 31st March 1982. If the shares are unquoted a price will have to be agreed with the Inland Revenue.

Now Step 2. This is the easy bit. The price per share will be clearly printed on your contract note.

Right, we are into the home straight now. *Step 3*. Indexation relief only goes back to March 1982. So on any purchases made before this date you calculate the rise in the retail prices index between March 1982 and the date of the sale. For shares bought after March 1982 you simply use the month in which the purchase was made as your base and work out the subsequent rise in the retail prices index to the month of sale.

Finally, you put all the information together. First, deduct your acquisition cost from the net sale proceeds. This will give you your gain or loss before applying the indexation allowance. Second, calculate the indexation allowance. You do this by using the formula below:

$$\frac{RD - RI}{RI}$$

Where RD = retail prices index for the month of disposal, RI = retail prices index for the month of acquisition or March 1982 whichever is the later.

You'll find the answer will be a decimal fraction, such as 0.1234. This is then rounded to the nearest third decimal place, i.e. 0.123. Third, you then multiply this figure by your acquisition cost to give you your indexation adjustment. On a profit this figure is used to reduce the gain and if there is a loss, the loss is increased.

Example A

You bought 50,000 shares at 25p in April 1983 and sold them for 100p in May 1985. The retail prices index stood at 332.5 in April 1983 and at 375.6 in May 1985.

Sale proceeds	£50,000
Acquisition cost	£12,500
Unindexed gain	£37,500

Indexation allowance

$$\frac{375.6 - 332.5}{332.5} = 0.130$$

$0.130 \times £12,500$	£ 1,625
Chargeable gain	£35,875

Example B

You bought 50,000 shares at 10p in May 1980 and sold them for 100p in May 1985. On 31st March 1982, the shares were 20p. The retail prices index stood at 313.4 in March 1982 and at 375.6 in May 1985.

Sale proceeds	£50,000
Cost of shares	£ 5,000
Unindexed gain	£45,000

Indexation allowance

$$\frac{375.6 - 313.4}{313.4} = 0.198$$

$0.198 \times £10,000$	£ 1,980
Chargeable gain	£43,020

Note: If you are calculating the indexation allowance on shares purchased before March 1982, then you adjust the formula accordingly.

RD = RPI for the month of disposal.

RI = RPI for March 1982.

The decimal fraction is then multiplied by the value as at 31st March 1982 as opposed to the actual cost.

Example C

You bought 50,000 shares at 25p in April 1983 and sold them for 20p in May 1985. The retail prices index stood at 332.5 in April 1983 and at 375.6 in May 1985.

Sale proceeds	£10,000
Acquisition cost	£12,500
Unindexed loss	£ 2,500
Indexation allowance	£ 1,625
Allowable loss	£ 4,125

74

Variations

If you have bought shares in the same company over a number of years, your local tax office will be able to give you details about how to calculate the indexation allowance.

Transferring the Allowance

It is not possible to transfer your indexation allowance due on disposal to another person, unless the transaction is completed between husband and wife. That's because under the current rules husband and wife are treated as a single unit for capital gains tax purposes.

If you make a gift of shares to someone other than your husband or wife, special rules apply. Your local inspector can fill in the details.

Employee Share Schemes

An increasing number of companies are either offering their employees the right to purchase shares in the company where they work at special rates or giving them shares as a free gift. Normally the Inland Revenue regards this perk as part of an employees' income and as such taxable at their rate of income tax. Tax is payable on the difference between the market value of shares and the price (if any) paid by the employee.

However, legislation has been introduced since 1978 to lighten this tax burden for schemes complying with certain fixed rules. Schemes which have been approved by the Inland Revenue give employees the chance to acquire shares without generating an immediate income tax liability, although they are liable to capital gains tax when they sell their shares if the gains for the year exceed their exemption. There are three types of approved scheme.

Profit Sharing Schemes
(Finance Act 1978)

Who can participate: Employees of five years standing. Those who have worked for a shorter period can be included at the company's discretion.

What are they given: Ordinary shares in the company. The annual limit is £1,250 or 10% of salary up to £5,000, whichever is the greater.

Restrictions: The shares must be held by trustees for two years except in certain compassionate circumstances such as death or redundancy.

Tax treatment: Dividends are subject to income tax but they have a tax credit attached which is equivalent to the payment of basic rate tax. If you sell the shares after two years, but less than four years, you pay income tax on either the value of the original shares or their sale price, whichever is less. If you wait until year five then your income tax bill is reduced by 25%, and once you reach year six, you can sell your shares with no income tax charge at all.

Savings Related Share Option Schemes (Finance Act 1980)

Who can participate: Employees of five years standing. Those who have worked for a shorter period can be included at the company's discretion.

What are they given: The right to buy at today's price shares on a future date. The employer can give a 10% discount on the current price of the shares.

Restrictions: The employee pays monthly contributions, maximum £100, under a save as you earn tax free contract normally for five years. At the end of this period the accumulated savings can be used to take up the shares at the price stated at the start.

Tax treatment: Dividends are subject to income tax. When you sell the shares there is a potential capital gains tax liability based on the actual price paid for the shares.

Share Option Schemes (Finance Act 1984)

Who can participate: At the company's discretion.

What are they given: The right to buy at today's price shares on a future date. No discount is permitted. The overall limit per employee is £100,000 or four times salary, whichever is the greater.

Restrictions: To obtain tax relief the employee must not exercise the option to buy shares more than once every three years.

Tax treatment: Dividends are subject to income tax. Provided the restrictions noted above are followed, no income tax is payable on the shares, but there is a potential capital gains tax liability on any profits realised when the shares are sold.

Chapter Fifteen
Investment Clubs

Investment clubs provide an informal and enjoyable means of investing in stocks and shares. Basically you'll need to find about a dozen people interested in becoming members who broadly share the same investment objectives. Each one must be prepared to devote a certain amount of time to researching companies which may be suitable investments and helping with the administration where necessary.

Setting Up a Club
The simplest and cheapest method of establishing an investment club is to form a partnership. Under current legislation, enshrined in the 1948 Companies Act, partnerships cannot exceed 20 members but this should not prove a handicap at least in the early days. Experience among investment clubs in this country and the USA suggests they work best when restricted to between ten and 15 members.

   If you are planning a membership of more than 20 then you will have to form and run a limited company. Start-up costs will be several hundred pounds and you will need to keep detailed accounts so that an annual audited report of the company's activities can be made to the Registrar of Companies.

First Meeting

Before setting up the first meeting write to the National Association of Investment Clubs Ltd, Halifax House, 5 Fenwick Street, Liverpool L2 0PR. They have prepared a detailed manual which includes draft agreements and draft rules for investment clubs. This is available price £5.50. Read the manual thoroughly and make sure you understand the contents. Then choose a name for the proposed club and type out a draft agenda. This should be circulated to all those attending the meeting.

Example of Draft Agenda for the Setting-Up of the Moneyspinners Investment Club

Draft agenda for the first meeting of the Moneyspinners Investment Club to be held at Number 1, The High Street, on 1st January 1985 at 6.00 pm.

- Election of Chairman.
- Discussion on formation of the Moneyspinners Investment Club.
- Vote on formation of above Club.
- Vote on draft agreement and rules of the Club.
- Sign agreement and rules of Club.
- First meeting of the Club.

Appoint chairman, treasurer and club secretary. Formally adopt rules. Discuss the appointment of nominee or trustee. Appoint bank, stockbroker and auditor. Arrange for first payments of members. Statement from treasurer on sum available for investment. Choose investment and discuss future strategy. Arrange date for next meeting.

The first meeting of the club is crucial and you may find you do not have sufficient time after the initial chat to complete all the formalities involved. Rather than rush matters, after agreeing to establish the club simply set a date for the first formal meeting.

In order for the club to prosper each member must be prepared to set aside a regular sum every month and spend some time helping to research companies considered investment candidates. In addition, someone who is good at handling figures will be needed to tackle the job of treasurer.

Organising the Shareholdings

One of the most critical decisions is how to organise the holding of the shares. Shares in this country can only be owned by individuals or corporate entities. That means Moneyspinner Investment Club cannot buy shares in its own name. This is not an insurmountable problem. There are three solutions:–

a) Appoint trustees from among the club members who can hold the stock.
b) Use a nominee.
c) Set up a limited company.

The easiest option is to use a nominee. A nominee is simply a company which for a fee will hold the stock on behalf of an individual, company or partnership. Nominees are often used when the real owner of the shares does not wish his identity to be public. The high street banks run nominee companies. They will handle the paperwork for you and arrange to pay any dividends into the club's bank account. They will also store the share certificates for a fee.

Appointing a trustee is another quite popular method but this can become rather complex if membership is changing. You could end up with stock registered in the name of a trustee who wishes to leave the club. Then you will have the hassle and extra expense of re-registering the stock. Finally, setting up a company is an expensive business and entails a whole set of legal and accounting requirements.

Arranging for Banking Facilities

Another vital decision is choosing a bank or building society account. There is not much point shopping around for the account paying the highest interest as you probably will not have much spare cash sitting uninvested. You should therefore go for a bank which offers free current account banking plus a full range of products including, if necessary, a nominee service.

The chairman and treasurer should arrange to meet the bank manager and explain the club's requirements in full.

For security purposes it is best to specify three club members who can sign cheques and agree that a minimum of two signatures is required. Once the bank account has been set up, individual members can arrange for monthly standing orders to cover their contributions.

Cost of using Bank Nominee Services

BANK	STOCK		HOLDING*
	In	Out	
† Bank of Scotland‡	£4	£4	£1.50 half yearly
Barclays	£5	£2.50	£5 per year
Lloyds	£10	£10	£2 per quarter
† Midland	£6	£6	£2 per quarter
Natwest	£6	£6	£2 half yearly
† Royal Bank of Scotland Group	£4	£4	£1 half yearly
† TSB	No fixed charge		Fees individually negotiated

* Holding charge for each stock held.

† These banks do not make charges on current accounts provided the account is in credit.

‡ Providing London nominee company is used.

VAT will be added to all charges.

Accounting

Care is needed to keep the accounts up to date and accurate. The manual supplied by the national association will provide more detailed help and if you are in any doubt it may be worth consulting an accountant.

Taxation

The same rules on tax apply to all investors whether your holdings are via an investment club or direct. It is therefore essential to include full details of your share in an investment club's portfolio when completing your tax form.

Chapter Sixteen
Leaving it to
the Professionals

If you don't want to choose your own shares, then there are
several ways of obtaining relatively cheap professional
advice. For newcomers to the stockmarket or those who wish
to invest overseas it may be helpful to delegate the buying
decisions on at least part of your portfolio. You can either opt
for an individual service from a stockbroker or a packaged
deal in the form of unit trusts, offshore funds or insurance
linked products.

Discretionary Service
Stockbrokers are in the business of buying and selling
shares and you will therefore find they usually have plenty
of ideas on what stocks you should be switching between at
any one time. However, they cannot keep in touch by phone
with all their clients and you may feel you would prefer a
more thorough service. Most brokers will for a fee take full
charge of your portfolio – buying and selling shares, handling the paperwork and presenting you with the appropriate
data for the taxman at the end of each financial year. Brokers
differ about the minimum amount of money they will con-

sider for this service, known as discretionary. A few years ago the amount averaged around £50,000 but now brokers are suddenly keen to woo the private client and many have reduced their starting figure to around £20,000.

Before opting for a discretionary service you need to be as sure as humanly possible that your broker is capable of providing both reliable financial advice and a first class administrative service. You should check the charges carefully and the security arrangements. Small details such as when dividend payments are entered into your account can be crucial. You should also be quite specific about the guidelines you lay down. If you want a low risk portfolio aimed at income, say so, and what's more put it in writing. On the other hand, if you want growth, let them know that specifically.

Packaged Deals

There are quite literally thousands of investment schemes which give you the opportunity to place some of your money in shares. Some are quite straight forward and simply involve small investors pooling their resources and delegating the investment decisions to a professional fund manager. Others are more complex and may consist of a bundle of services ranging from life assurance through health insurance and investment in property, shares, cash and gilts.

When choosing between packages it is important to make sure you know exactly what you are buying:–
1. Who will be managing the money? What sort of experience do they have? What track record?
2. How safe is my money? Is this a high risk investment? What rules are there about where my money will be invested?
3. Can I get my money back straight away? If so, on what terms? Are there any tax implications depending upon when I want my money returned?
4. What charges are involved? What percentage of my money will be invested?
5. What is the tax position?

If you are simply looking for someone else to build up a share portfolio on your behalf, then it is best to concentrate upon three types of investment: unit trusts, investment trusts and offshore funds. Each of these provides a relatively cheap and simple way for you to buy high quality investment advice.

Unit Trusts

Who runs them? The unit trust group in conjunction with a trustee, usually a bank or insurance company. The unit trust group is responsible for the management of the funds, the marketing of the trust and the sale and purchase of units in the trust to the public. The trustee controls the purse strings, administers the cash and shares of the trust and makes certain the managers keep to the investment rules specified in the trust deed.

Who owns them? The unit holders whose money they invest.

Who regulates them? The Department of Trade regulates unit trusts extremely closely. It has rules about who can manage the trust, who can act as a trustee, how the units in the trust are priced and sold to the public and how the money in the trust is invested.

Investment restrictions: Trusts can invest in stocks and shares, gilts, and to a lesser extent, options. They cannot buy property, gold, commodities or deal in futures or currencies.

How to invest: Units are bought and sold by the managers. They are available direct from the managers or via intermediaries such as stockbrokers, licensed dealers in securities or members of the National Association of Security Dealers and Investment Managers.

Charges: There is no fixed level of charges. An initial charge is usually deducted from your investment and then there is an annual charge which is subtracted from the trust's assets. The standard initial charge is currently 5% and the annual charge varies from ½% to 1½%, with fees at the top end of the range being more common on overseas trusts.

There is also 1% stamp duty on the purchase of new units, plus ¼% unit trust instrument duty. You don't have to worry about paying these separately as the cost of all the charges is reflected in the price of the units you buy.

Pricing: The price of each unit is tied to the value of the underlying share portfolio. If this rises by 10% then the price of each unit should rise by 10%. The Department of Trade lays down exact rules on pricing to try to ensure fair play among all investors: new ones, existing unit holders and those wishing to cash in their units. Unit trust groups can calculate the value of the trust's share portfolio either on an offer basis or a bid basis. The offer basis assumes the highest possible price for the shares and usually reflects the cost of buying the particular shares. The bid basis assumes the lowest possible value for the share portfolio and reflects the return if the shares were sold. Most of the time the units are priced on an offer basis and managers are loath to switch onto a bid basis as this will lower the price of the units held by existing investors and make the fund's investment performance look bad. However, if there is a steady stream of money leaving the trust it would be unfair to the remaining investors if the trust was still priced on the higher offer basis. So in limited circumstances managers will switch the basis of calculation onto a bid price or halfway between bid and offer.

Liquidity: Most unit trusts are priced every day. You should have no problem buying or selling units at the quoted prices. However, if you wish to sell a large holding of say £10,000 in one day you may find some groups slightly lower the price they are prepared to pay. There is no standard practice on this matter, so check before hand.

Safety: The trustee is in a prime position to protect investor's interests and there have been no cases of investors money going astray since unit trusts were first set up in 1933. Of course, the risk of the investment decisions being unwise and the value of your units falling remains.

Tax: You receive dividends net of standard rate tax. Higher rate taxpayers will have a further tax bill. Non-taxpayers can reclaim any tax paid. There is a potential capital gains tax liability on profits from the sale of units.

Minimum investment: For lump sums the minimum ranges

from £200 to £1,000. For regular monthly payments the minimum can be as low as £20.

Choice: There are more than 730 unit trusts available. They range from funds aimed at income seekers, those looking for growth plus specialist overseas trusts.

Investment Trusts

Who runs them? Investment trusts are companies run by directors. It is the directors responsibility to plan all aspects of the company's management from investing its cash to organising its finances.

Who owns them? Shareholders.

Who regulates them? As companies, investment trusts have to comply with company law and if their shares are quoted on the Stock Exchange they must satisfy the Exchange's own requirements.

Investment restrictions: In order to qualify for certain tax concessions, investment trusts must comply with rules laid down by the Inland Revenue regarding, for example, the percentage of their portfolio invested in any one share. That aside, they are free to invest in whatever they wish.

How to invest: Shares in quoted investment trusts can be bought or sold through a stockbroker or licensed dealer in securities.

Charges: The charges are exactly the same as those involved in buying any parcel of shares from a broker. They consist of brokers commission based on the size of the transaction, 1% stamp duty, contract note stamp and the Council for Securities levy. On sales there is no stamp duty.

Pricing: The price of shares in an investment trust reflects the supply and demand for its shares. It does not move in direct line with changes in the underlying value of the share portfolio. This means the share price can either stand at a premium or a discount to the worth of the company's investment. In recent years the share price of many investment trusts has been at a substantial discount to the real value of the investments held by the company. This has led to a spate of takeovers and some trusts have been turned into unit trusts, which more accurately reflect the value of its investments.

Liquidity: Provided the investment trust has a full quote, is reasonably large and its shares are widely held it should be easy to buy and sell shares through a broker without forcing the price sharply up or down. Before investing in a particular trust do ask your broker how wide the market is in its shares.

Safety: As with any stock market investment you are placing your money in the hands of the company's directors. On the investment front the share price will reflect both the managers actual performance and the market's expectation about future profits growth.

Tax: As with shares. Dividends are paid net of standard rate tax but subject to income tax at your rate. Any gains on share sales are liable to capital gains tax.

Minimum: Under existing commission structures investors with less than £1,000 to invest may find this relatively expensive, although it will be cheaper than opting for a unit trust.

Choice: There are over 200 quoted investment trusts. The choice is slightly more limited than for unit trusts, but mainstream investment needs for income, growth and overseas shares are well covered.

Offshore Funds

Who runs them? The fund managers in conjunction with a custodian, such as a bank or insurance company. The division of responsibility between the fund manager and the custodian is the same as between the fund manager of a unit trust and the trustee.

Who owns them? Unit holders or shareholders whose money they invest.

Who regulates them? The governing authority at the offshore centre where the company is incorporated.

Investment restrictions? None, except where specified in the fund's prospectus.

How to invest: Units are bought and sold by the managers. Information about these funds can only be obtained by private individuals through their financial advisers. Some funds have circumvented this restriction by obtaining a stock market quote for their shares, so they can then advertise a prospectus in this country.

Charges: There are no fixed charges. Some funds such as currency deposit funds may have no initial charge while others may charge as much as 7½%. Annual charges also vary. Some funds levy an exit fee rather than an initial charge.

Pricing: There are no fixed rules. Read the small print carefully. Some funds may base their prices directly on net asset value at all times, other may be free to choose between several methods of calculation.

Liquidity: Many offshore funds only buy and sell units or shares once a week or even once a month. Check in advance. The fund managers may, in certain circumstances, exercise the right to suspend repayment for up to six months. Read the small print with great care.

Safety: Standard of regulation in offshore centres varies tremendously. Unfortunately, in a number of cases it is not as high as that of our own Department of Trade.

Tax: Dividends are paid gross and you must settle your own income tax. Capital gains tax is liable on any gains made on the sale of units or shares unless you simply swop one class of shares in a company for another. This loophole has been used to full advantage by several fund managers who now run offshore umbrella funds offering investors the chance to switch tax free betwen different sub-funds which in turn invest in shares, bonds and currencies.

Minimum investment: Varies from £500 – £2,500.

Choice: Wide range of funds investing in shares, currencies, bonds, property and commodities.

Section II

A

Account

When you buy shares you don't have to pay for them straight away. The Stock Exchange divides the year up into 24 so-called accounts, each of which normally lasts two weeks. Shares bought during an account must be paid for within ten days of the account ending. This means you have up to three weeks free credit before having to settle your bill. If you buy and sell within an account you can cut down on charges. You save on stamp duty and halve your commission costs.

Account Day

The day of reckoning when buyers of shares have to settle their bills is known as the account or settlement day. It is usually the second Monday after the end of an account.

Accumulation Units

There are two types of units available in most unit trusts. These are accumulation and income units. Accumulation units are designed for investors who do not wish to receive dividend cheques. Instead the dividends minus basic rate tax are rolled up into the price of the units. That's why if you look at tables of units trust prices you will often find two different prices for units in a single trust. The accumulation units will stand at a higher price than the income units. Holders of income units receive a stream of dividends, usually twice a year.

Advisory Service

An increasing number of stockbrokers are wooing the private investor. One of the services they offer is called 'advisory'. As its name suggests this boils down to the broker suggesting share purchases to the customer but leaving the ultimate decision in the hands of the individual investor. There is usually no fee charged for this service as the broker will earn commission every time you buy or sell shares.

After Hours Dealing

Just as the banks close their doors to the public before teatime, so the Stock Exchange shuts up shop for the day at 3.30 pm. You can buy shares after 3.30 pm but they will count as the first deals done on the following day. These transactions are sometimes called early bargains.

Agent

The agent is an intermediary or third party, such as an insurance broker, who sells the products of several companies. A large proportion of unit trust sales in this country are completed by agents, who in turn are paid commission for their trouble by the groups whose merchandise they sell.

Agreed Bid

More often than not bids are acrimonious affairs with the company being taken over fighting tooth and nail to maintain its independence. Sometimes, however, the terms of the would-be purchaser are regarded as sufficiently attractive to the board of the target company that they are prepared to recommend the bid to shareholders. The offer then becomes an agreed bid. If you hold shares in a company which is the subject of an agreed bid you will receive a letter from the bidder stating the terms on which they will buy your shares and also a recommendation from the directors to accept the bid. It always pays to wait until the last minute before accepting the terms offered, although in the case of an agreed bid it is unlikely that a better offer will be made.

Allotment Letter

This is a letter from a company saying that you own a certain number of shares. You will come across this bit of paper if you take up what is called a new issue, when a company comes to the market for the first time, or if a company whose shares you already own wants to raise more money by increasing the number of its shares. You can sell the shares allocated to you in the allotment letter through your broker. There is no stamp duty and a reduced commission is usually charged.

Annual General Meeting

Once a year shareholders get a brief opportunity to question the board of directors and go over the company's figures for the previous year. Shareholders must be given at least 21 days notice along with a copy of the report and accounts. At the meeting they will be asked to approve the report and accounts, the election or re-election of directors and the appointment of the auditors.

Annual Report

The basic document by which shareholders can examine the trading and financial strength of the company. Each report begins with a statement from the directors summarising developments during the year and outlining future prospects. A profit and loss account shows the results of the company's trading over the year. A balance sheet at year-end, essentially a snap shot of the company's finances taken on a specific date. Plus a statement on funding, showing how the company financed its business and the use made of the money. At the end of this document you should find a brief but vital paragraph written and signed by the auditors stating that the figures show what is called a true and fair view of the company's financial position.

All Share Index

The Financial Times Actuaries All Shares Index is a useful guide to movements in the stockmarket. It covers 750 major UK industrial, commercial and financial companies. It is calculated between 2.30 and 3.00 pm each day and then adjusted for late price movements. Finally, it is produced just after 6.00 pm.

Application Form

When a company wishes to sell shares to the public direct it will issue a detailed report of its activities, known as a prospectus. This will include an official application form for investors keen to buy shares. If you wish to buy shares you must fill in the application form and then cut it out and return the form to the specified address. Photocopies of the form are not accepted.

Authorised Share Capital

This figure is effectively the ceiling for the amount of capital a company can raise. It is usually substantially higher than the actual capital injected into the business which is referred to as paid-up capital.

Authorised Unit Trusts

Before a unit trust can be marketed to the public in this country it must be vetted by the Department of Trade to ensure that the company running the fund is suitable and that the trust itself conforms to current rules. Only once a trust has the Department of Trade's seal of good housekeeping can advertisements for it be placed in the newspapers.

B

Back to Back Loans

A tool used by unit trusts with overseas portfolios who think that the currency in which they have invested is about to weaken against sterling. In order to prevent what it considers to be currency speculation the Department of Trade will only allow unit trust managers to use back to back loans as a method of protecting foreign shares against adverse currency movements. As the name suggests two transactions are involved. First, the group deposits sterling with a bank and then it arranges to borrow the equivalent amount in foreign currency. This allows the fund managers to lock in their commitments at a specific exchange rate.

Balance Sheet

A crucial element in every company's annual report. The balance sheet shows the financial affairs of the company on the day specified. It will indicate the impact of the previous year's trading on the company's financial health. It can also be used to estimate future trends as it will include details of money owed and due in the near future.

Bargain

The name given to a transaction on the Stock Exchange. It does not imply that the share purchase or sale was carried out at a relatively cheap price.

Bear

The origin of the term is shrouded in mystery but it refers to someone who thinks either the market or a specific share is likely to fall in price.

Bearer Stocks

Stocks where the sole proof of ownership is holding the certificate itself. No record is kept of the shareholders.

Bed and Breakfast

This is the phrase used when a share is sold and then bought back the next day. The aim of the double transaction being to establish a disposal for capital gains tax purposes. The introduction of indexation of capital gains has reduced the popularity for this procedure.

Bid Price

The price at which you can sell either shares or unit trusts. It is lower than what is called the offer price – which is the amount you would have to pay if you wished to buy the shares or units.

Bid

When a company wishes to purchase another company it makes what is called a bid. This will detail the price it is willing to pay and specify whether the offer is cash, shares or a mixture. Shareholders in companies on the receiving end of a bid should not act hastily. Frequently, the opening offer is subsequently increased and you should wait until the final day of the offer before accepting.

Blue Button
The name given to employees of stock broking firms who work on the floor of the Stock Exchange. Their job is to check prices. After a few years they may be promoted to 'Authorised Dealers' who can then deliver orders for the sale or purchase of shares.

Blue Chip
The phrase originated in the USA. It refers to companies of exceptional standing. These companies are not necessarily the best investments as often they are past their peak in terms of earnings expansion but they have excellent management, quality products and proven track records.

Book
The name given to the stock of units or shares held by the unit trust managers or jobbers.

Bonus Issue
The terms bonus, scrip, capitalisation and free issue are used interchangeably. In fact, shareholders strictly speaking are not getting something for nothing. The new shares simply represent a transfer of money from the companies reserves to its permanent capital. Generally, the existing share price should fall to compensate for the new shares and keep the company's stock market value the same.

Bull
The term used to describe a person who thinks a market or share is due to rise. The opposite of bear.

Business Expansion Scheme
In 1983 the Thatcher government introduced the Business Expansion Scheme which was intended to encourage individuals to invest in high risk companies which are not quoted on the stock exchange. As an incentive you can obtain in-

come tax relief on investments of up to £40,000. For the higher rate taxpayer these schemes make excellent sense provided due care is taken when choosing your investments. Professional advice from an accountant or stockbroker is recommended. The current scheme runs until April 1987.

C

Call
A request for cash to be paid on shares. For example, some companies such as mining or oil exploration firms, issue shares at below par value and later on call upon existing shareholders to pay more. If the shares at £1 were sold for 40p, then the company could ask shareholders to pay another 60p. If they refused they would forfeit the shares. A similar procedure is sometimes used with new issues, the most prominent recent example being British Telecom. In this case a price above par is fixed as the sale price, and payment is divided into instalments. Whoever owns the shares when the instalment is due has a responsibility to pay or else they will forfeit the shares.

Call Option
The right to buy a security for a fixed price within a specified period.

Capital
The money put into a business by its shareholders is described as its capital. The phrase 'working capital' is used to indicate the available resources for a company to fund its current operations.

Capitalisation Issue
See bonus issue.

Capital Gains Tax
Individuals who make a profit from selling a capital asset such as shares, jewellery or a second home must pay tax on any gains over and above the standard allowance. For the

year 1985-6 this allowance is £5,900. So by careful timing of the scale of crucial items most people should be able to avoid a capital gains tax bill. Since 1982 investors have also been allowed to increase the original cost of their shares to keep pace with inflation.

Cash Settlement
When you buy government securities, traded options and new issues you have to pay cash. Indeed with new issues you may find yourself temporarily out of pocket as it can take days before you get your cheque returned if you are unsuccessful in applying for shares. Sometimes your cheque is cashed although you don't receive all the shares you asked for. In these cases the speed with which your money returns depends upon the efficiency of the merchant bank handling the new issue.

Chartist
There are as many theories about the movement in share prices as you have probably had hot dinners. Many are based on assembling and analysing a vast array of technical data and then isolating what are regarded as key variables such as debt and profitability. Particularly popular at the moment are those analysts who use charts to plot the movements in share prices and try to predict floors and ceilings from these. Although these give a superficial aura of scientific authenticity, in the end it all boils down to individual interpretation of the data.

Circular
A document sent to shareholders in a company by the directors when a major change in the nature of the business or its share structure is envisaged. Details of the time and place of an extraordinary general meeting to vote on the contents of the circular will be included.

Cold Call
If you receive an unsolicited approach from someone trying to sell you shares or unit trusts then this is a cold call and it is illegal. You should report the call to the Department of

Trade. The government is currently considering changing the rules to allow cold calling on unit trusts but first it has to be satisfied that investors interests will be fully protected.

Commission
Brokers earn commission on the majority of share deals. This is normally 1.65% of the price of the transaction. However, on small purchases or sales most brokers charge a flat fee of between £10 and £20, while for larger deals the cost decreases. On unit trusts, an initial charge – usually 5% – is deducted from investors' capital to cover marketing and administration. Out of this 3% is paid by Unit Trust Association members to recognised intermediaries who finalise sales of unit trusts. Non-members of the Unit Trust Association may pay higher commissions.

Compensation Fund
The Compensation Fund is run by the Stock Exchange. The aim is to protect users of the system if a broker or jobber goes bust. Originally it was an independent fund topped up as required by individual members. In the mid-1970's the Stock Exchange itself took over the fund and it is financed out of its own budget. Ultimately its size is virtually unlimited as if a major crisis arose the Stock Exchange can call upon the member firms and finally on the personal assets of individual members.

Concert Party
The name given to two or more shareholders who are regarded by the authorities, in the shape of the Take Over Panel, as acting together or 'in concert'. Their shareholdings are added together and have to be declared if they exceed 5%. Similarly if their aggregate holdings total more than 29.9% they have to bid for the rest of the shares.

Contract Note
This is similar to a receipt from a store. When you buy or sell shares your broker will send you a contract note confirming the transactions, specifying the shares, number, price, date and cost. This should be kept safely as it will be essential

when you come to fill in your tax form that you have proof of the exact purchase or sale price and date. It should not be confused with the share certificate which will be despatched several weeks later by the company itself.

Convertible
A hybrid between a share and a fixed rate stock. It is a fixed interest stock which guarantees the holder the right to buy a certain number of shares at a specified date in the future. The most common types of convertibles are convertible loan stock which pays interest gross and convertible preference stock which pays interest net. They are a useful way for investors seeking reasonably high income to obtain a limited exposure to the growth potential in the ordinary share.

Corporation Stocks
These are fixed rate stocks offered by local authorities and indeed some cities. They usually pay higher interest than the equivalent stock issued by the government.

Coupon
A detachable portion of a bond or share certificate which must be sent to the issuing house or company which is administering the payment of interest or dividends on the stock. It is proof of ownership of the stock in those cases where the certificates are not recorded centrally.

Cum
Old Latin hands will know that cum means 'with'. So when you buy shares or units cum distribution you are also buying the right to receive dividends. Shares are also sold cum rights and cum scrip with the entitlement to buy the rights or receive the scrip.

Cumulative Preference Shares
The shares give the holder the right to receive outstanding dividend payments which were not paid in the past. It effectively puts the holder at the front of the queue ahead of ordinary shareholders.

Current Cost Accounting

Rampaging inflation in the seventies led to the introduction of a new system of accounting which would reflect the impact of inflation on a company's balance sheet.

Current Yield

The interest or dividends due in one year expressed as a percentage of the price of the stock or shares. The yield is usually quoted gross, that's before any tax has been deducted. That does not necessarily mean it will be paid gross. Dividends on ordinary shares are paid net of standard tax but shareholders who do not pay tax can reclaim the tax paid on their behalf. For example, if you buy stock at £100 and receive £10 interest then the yield is 10%. If you bought the same stock at £50 and received £10 interest, then the yield would rise to 20%.

D

Dawn Raid

The name given when a potential buyer of a large parcel of shares in a company tries to build up a sizeable holding in a single swoop. Called dawn raid as the manoeuvre usually takes place as soon as business starts in the morning.

Dealing

The term used to describe transactions in stocks and shares.

Dealing for New Time

During the final two days of an account shares can be bought for the following account. If you wish to do this, you must say so at the outset. You will be charged a slightly higher price for this transaction, but of course you get a further 20 days in which to pay.

Debenture

A fixed rate stock which is usually secured against the company's assets. It ranks ahead of the ordinary shares if a company is wound up. It is quoted in units of £100.

Debt

Money owed by a company to its creditors. The phrase debt service ratio is sometimes used. This indicates the ease or difficulty which a company faces in paying the interest on its debt. *Derivatives - instrument To hedge - exposures - very very risky indeed*

Dictum Meum Pactum

My word is my bond. The operating motto of the Stock Exchange where huge transactions are concluded by word of mouth.

Discretionary

Some brokers offer their customers what is called a discretionary service. The investor gives his or her broker a free hand to buy and sell stocks and shares. Do be careful before agreeing to such an arrangement that you are dealing with a bone fide adviser, with sound financial credentials and that you have a formal agreement specifying the range of investments in which your money can be channelled.

Discount

You will often read about shares trading at a discount. This means that the share price does not fully reflect the value of the company as set out in its accounts. Many property companies and investment trusts frequently trade at substantial discounts to the value of their assets. The term is also used when the price of one class of shares is less than another. For example most companies make rights issues at discounts to the ordinary shares as they anticipate the share price falling to accommodate the new shares.

Distribution Date

The date when interest or dividends are distributed to stock and share owners. Usually twice a year.

Distributor Status

A relative newcomer to the money dictionary. It refers to offshore funds which have passed the Inland Revenue's rules on distributing the bulk of their gains. It is only granted on an annual basis and retrospectively after the Revenue has considered that year's trading. It means that when unit holders come to sell their units the gains are subject to capital gains tax. If a fund does not qualify then gains on its units are subject to income tax.

Dividend
Payment made to shareholders usually out of the group's previous year's earnings. Dividends are paid net of tax but non-taxpayers can reclaim the tax paid on their behalf. Companies decide the level of dividends they wish to pay after they have seen their half year or full year results.

Dividend Cover
The term used to describe the number of times in theory a company could afford to pay out a given level of dividend. For example, if this is less than one it cannot afford to maintain the dividend at current levels.

E

Earnings per Share
When assessing the value of a share a critical figure is the earnings per share. This is simply the companies total earnings after tax and prior claims divided by the number of shares in issue.

Equity
The residue after all other claims have been settled is the equity and it is equally owned by all ordinary shareholders in proportion to their holdings.

Ex
From the Latin 'without'. When you buy shares ex-dividend it means you are not entitled to the dividend. Also common, ex-rights and ex-scrip.

Exempt
Certain funds and gilts are called exempt. These are only

available to non-taxpayers such as charities and pension funds as the funds themselves are tax free.

Extraordinary General Meeting

A special meeting of shareholders is required when a company wishes to make a major purchase, disposal or alter its capital structure. Shareholders will receive full details of the proposal and the venue for the meeting in a circular.

Extraordinary Profit or Loss

This is a one-off profit or loss not related to the company's normal trading. For instance, the profit on the sale of some land may be considered an extraordinary profit by a manufacturer.

F

Fixed Interest Security

A stock which pays investors a fixed rate of interest. The actual return to investors will depend upon the price which they paid for the stock.

Floor

The name used to refer to the Stock Exchange's trading premises. Access to the floor is restricted and members of the public are not admitted. Instead they have to deal indirectly through a stockbroker.

Financial Year

Not necessarily twelve months but usually a calendar year Companies can choose for themselves when they wish to start their trading year. So-called half-year results do not have to cover six months and some retailers produce half-year figures for just three months trading.

Flotation

When a company's shares are sold on the stock market for the first time it is called a flotation. Also referred to as a new issue.

FTSE 100

An index of one hundred stocks which was introduced in January 1984 to complement the smaller FT Ordinary Index and the larger FT All Share Index. It provides a minute by minute picture of how the market is moving.

Financial Times Industrial Ordinary Index

Now 50 years old this index, sometimes referred to as the 30 Share Index or FT Index, is one way to monitor daily price movements. It is calculated hourly and provides a quick rule of thumb gauge for share watchers.

Futures

A contract to buy or sell a certain commodity at a fixed price at a specified date in the future.

G

Gearing

A company with nil gearing is one with no borrowings which is financed solely out of its cash or money from shareholders. The level of gearing represents the amount a company has borrowed expressed as a percentage of its share capital.

Gilts or Gilt Edged

These are fixed rate stocks issued and guaranteed by the UK government. You can buy them from your stockbroker and about half of those issued are available through the post office.

Golden Handshake

Lump sum payments made to departing key executives have come to be known in the popular press as golden handshakes.

Government Broker

Is appointed by the governor of the Bank of England after consultation with the Stock Exchange. Traditionally a member of the Stock Exchange, the government broker handles the daily marketing of gilts.

Gross
This means that no tax has been deducted. For example, gilts bought on the National Savings Stock Register pay interest gross while the same gilt held by the Bank of England will pay investors net of standard rate tax.

Growth Stocks
These are shares in companies which are expected to grow faster than the average. As a result they usually pay very small dividends. Often they are small to medium sized companies in expanding markets or sectors currently regarded by investors as glamorous.

H

Hammer
On the rare occasion that a member of the Stock Exchange goes bust they are hammered. The official ritual which consists of ringing a bell three times and making a brief announcement takes place on the floor of the Exchange. It marks their expulsion from the ranks of stock market members. Clients of the former member are usually directed by the Stock Exchange to another member and throughout a clients money is protected by the compensation fund.

Hedge
To protect. This is normally used in reference to protecting currency gains as in 'hedging against the dollar' but it can simply refer to hedging gains in a share price. Various methods of hedging are available to private and institutional investors. These include using options, futures and back-to-back loans.

Historic Cost Accounting
The phrase used to describe the traditional method of drawing up a company's account. This has now been augmented

by the introduction of current cost accounting which attempts to account for the impact of inflation.

Holdings
Another term for share stake. The diminutive of share-holdings.

I

Income
The money shareholders receive by way of dividends is referred to as income. It is taxable at their level of income tax. Shares with above average yields are referred to as income stocks.

Income Units
These are units in a unit trust which distribute their dividends to investors. They are contrasted with accumulation units which roll up the dividends into the unit price.

Indexation
The adjustment of a price to take account of inflation, usually as measured by the Retail Prices Index. In March 1983 the government introduced indexation of capital gains so investors no longer need to pay tax on inflationary gains.

Index-Linked Gilts
In 1982 the government introduced a new type of gilt. Both the interest payments and the eventual capital repayments are guaranteed to rise (or fall) in line with the Retail Prices Index.

Initial Yield
The yield when a share or unit trust is first launched, based on its issue price.

Introduction
Shares in a company new to the market are offered to the public in the normal way through stockbrokers and jobbers.

This is the least formal method of bringing a new company to the market and is often used when large multinationals are first quoted in London.

Investment Trust

A company which invests in other companies. It is a relatively cheap way for individuals and institutions to obtain professional management of a portfolio of shares. Full details of the investment trusts which are members of the Association of Investment Trust Companies are to be found in section six. The price of shares in an investment trust quoted on the stock exchange will depend upon the supply and demand for its shares but usually moves in line with the rise or fall of the underlying share portfolio. Unlike unit trusts, investment trusts can borrow money and have greater freedom to invest in a wide range of securities, options, futures and commodities. They can be purchased through a stockbroker and the charges are the same as on standard share transactions.

Issuing House

The name given to the company, usually a merchant bank, which masterminds a new issue. It is responsible for launching and marketing the new shares and in return is paid a fee by the company whose securities it is selling.

J

Jobber

At the moment stockbrokers cannot actually buy and sell shares without going to a jobber. When a broker wishes to buy some shares he or his representative will go onto the floor of the Stock Exchange and walk round the various booths manned by several firms of jobbers. He will tell them what share he wishes to deal in but will not say whether he is a buyer or a seller. The jobber will quote two prices – one at which he is prepared to supply stock and the other at which he is happy to take up the shares. The distinction between the jobber and broker is likely to evaporate in 1986 when new rules governing the running of the market are introduced.

Jobbers Turn

This is the difference between the buying and selling price quoted by the jobber. On large stocks which are easy to deal in this turn is usually around 2% but on smaller stocks, or those where the price is displaying sudden unexpected movements the spread is wider.

L

Licensed Dealer in Securities

At the moment in order to sell securities – that's shares and unit trusts – companies must either be stockbrokers, banks, members of the trade association NASDIM (National Association of Security Dealers and Investment Managers) or licensed by the Department of Trade as bona fide dealers. Under the government's current proposals on investor protection the department of trade will delegate its responsibilities in this area to self regulatory bodies composed of financial institutions. In the meantime, if you wish to check whether a company does hold a license then a list is available from HMSO, PO Box 276, London SW8. Price £6.30.

Listed Company

A company with a full quote on the Stock Exchange. There are currently about 7,000 listed companies and details of the share prices of the main ones can be found in the financial pages of the quality national papers.

Loan Stock

An IOU from a company to an investor guaranteeing to pay a given rate of interest and return the capital intact on a given date.

Longs

The term used to describe gilts with a maturity of more than 15 years.

M

Member Firm

A fully fledged member of the Stock Exchange whose activities are covered by the Compensation Fund and whose staff has passed the Stock Exchange exams.

Medium

The term used to describe gilts with a maturity of between five and fifteen years.

Merger

When two companies agree to form a single corporation.

Middle Price

This is the price usually found in the newspaper columns. It is halfway between the price the jobber is prepared to buy and sell shares, e.g. Newspaper price 100p; Bid or selling price 99p; Offer or buying price 101p.

Marketing of Investments Board Organising Committee (MIBOC)

Set up in 1985 in preparation for the government's new proposals on investor protection and its desire for the financial community to regulate itself. Under the chairmanship of Mark Weinberg it is currently working its way through a series of issues effecting the marketing of investments including, commissions and licensing of all insurance salesmen. It's long-term future is not guaranteed and it may well be merged into the Securities and Investment Board.

Minorities

The term used to describe outside shareholders in a subsidiary of another company.

Mortgage Debenture

A loan secured against the asset of a property. It usually ranks ahead of both debenture holders and ordinary shareholders.

N

NASDIM

The National Association of Security Dealers and Investment Managers consists of a broad range of companies ranging from some of the financial industry's giants through to its minnows. Membership can be checked at its headquarters in 28 Lovat Lane, London EC3R 1HP. At present there is no compensation fund in place for its members.

NSSR

The National Savings Stock Register shows which gilts are available from the post office. For small investors wishing to buy less than £1,000 it is cheaper to buy at your post office than from a broker.

Net Assets

The sum of money available to ordinary shareholders in the event of the company being wound up. This is sometimes expressed in relation to the number of shares as 'net asset per share'. If you see a company where net assets per share are substantially above the share price you should try to find out more. It may be that the market doubts the value of the assets and thinks they would not realise as much as the accounts suggest. Alternatively, the company could be starting to recover after a rough period and may present an attractive investment opportunity.

Net Profit

The profit after tax, interest, extraordinary items and payment to minorities. Net attributable profit is the sum available for shareholders and is assessed after deductions have also been made for dividends.

New Issue

Shares from a company coming to the market for the first time. There is no commission payable on purchases of a new issue but you do have to pay cash up front. If you are allocated shares, you will receive an allotment letter and several weeks later a share certificate.

Nil Paid Shares

You will probably come across this term when a company is raising extra cash through a rights issue. It will issue nil paid shares and fix a date on which these shares must be paid for. The shares can be traded in the market and may change hands for several pence.

Nominal

The face value of a stock or share. It is of academic interest.

Nominee

This is usually a company but it could refer to a person or firm who acts on behalf of a third party who may not wish to have their identity revealed.

O

OTC

Over-the-Counter. This is the unregulated market in shares run outside the auspices of the Stock Exchange by dealers in licensed securities. Often the dealer will both bring a new issue to the OTC market, take a fee from the company and then make a market in the shares. The potential conflicts of interest are legion and investors should treat such issues with extreme caution.

Offer Price

The price at which a jobber or unit trust manager is prepared to sell shares or units.

Offer for Sale

When shares in a company new to the market are offered to the public at a fixed price.

Official List

The Stock Exchange publishes a daily official list quoting all the dealings in shares transacted each day.

Offshore

Outside the jurisdiction of the UK tax authorities. Offshore funds, in contrast to authorised unit trusts, cannot be marketed freely in the UK. They usually pay dividends gross before tax and their fee structure varies.

Options

The right to buy or sell a share at a given price within a certain period. These can be used either to protect gains made on existing shares or for speculative purposes. The price of options tends to move more quickly and dramatically than the share itself, so you need to be in close contact with your broker and the market.

Ordinary Shares

These are shares which entitle the holders to a proportion of the company's earnings and assets after any prior claims have been settled.

P

Par

The face value of a share or fixed interest stock. The par value of gilts for example is £100, while most UK companies set the par value of their ordinary shares at 25p. Under British law a company must set a par value on its ordinary shares but in some countries shares can have no par value, abbreviated to npv. The term nominal is used interchangeably with par in this context.

PLC

Public Limited Company.

Partly Paid

All shares must be given a par value but when they are sold to the public individual investors may only be asked to pay a portion of that par value straight away and be required to pay the rest at a later date fixed at the outset. This is not very common but may be a tactic used by a company seeking to raise substantial sums of money either in a new issue, such as British Telecom, or a rights issue, such as the Hanson Trust rights in July 1985. The term can also be applied to allotment letters in a rights issue before the cash has been paid.

P/E
Price earnings ratio. This is calculated by dividing a company's earnings per share into its share price. This is a crucial ratio used by analysts of shares. The higher the figure, the more highly rated the company. It can be used to help compare two companies in the same sector or the relative ratings of several sectors. However, as an investment tool it is only as good as the basic data which goes to make up the figures. Particularly crucial is the assumption made about tax. Some people calculate the p/e on the basis of actual tax paid that year, while others try to adjust the tax bill to iron out temporary fluctuations. Prospective p/e's are based on estimates of future earnings per share.

PEPS Personal Equity Plans (ie personal share portfolios)

Perks
Also known as freebies. These are special concessions for shareholders. A full list of share perks is available on pages 159 to 177.

Placing
When a broker or merchant bank advising a company arranges for institutions or individuals to buy that company's shares at a fixed price. This procedure cuts out the middle man or jobber. It is often used when there are a relatively small number of shares available in a new issue or alternatively when a sizeable stake in a company is for sale.

Portfolio
The collective noun for shares and securities.

Preference Share
A share which usually qualifies for a fixed dividend and whose holder will be repaid in advance of ordinary shareholders should the company be wound up or go into liquidation.

Privatisation
The sale of nationalised assets to the public.

Premium
An excess, usually used to describe a share price which stands above a particular benchmark such as assets per share or new issue price.

Prospectus
The document which companies are required to produce when making an issue of shares to the public. It gives information about the company's finances, previous track record, management, current business activities and future prospects. A copy of the prospectus must be lodged with the Registrar of Companies before shares in a new issue can be sold to the public.

Proxy
If a shareholder cannot be present at a meeting where a crucial vote is taking place, he can appoint a proxy to vote on his behalf.

Put Option
The right to sell a specific share at an agreed price within a stated period.

Put-through
When a stockbroker has matched a buyer and seller for a parcel of shares he can arrange for the two transactions to be completed by the jobber. This twinning arrangement is known as a put-through. It can save both a buyer and a seller money because the usual difference between the bid and offer price of a share is narrowed.

Q

Quoted
The old term for a company listed on the Stock Exchange.

Qualified Accounts

The term used to describe accounts which the auditors are unable to say represent a true and fair view of the company's position. A warning signal for shareholders that the company may be in trouble.

R

Ramp

Concerted or heavy buying of a share with the aim of artificially pushing up its price.

Redemption Date

Most commonly associated with gilts. It is the date at which the stock will be repaid at face value.

Redemption Yield

This is the yield an investor would receive assuming he or she held the stock until it was redeemed. If the stock is standing below par then it will include a capital gain and be higher than the flat yield.

Registered Stock

Most shares in the UK are registered, which means that companies can keep track of their shareholders. When you buy a share, your name is added to the register and the company will send you a certificate of ownership.

Rights Issue

When a company wishes to raise additional money it may decide to give its existing shareholders the first chance to support it further. It will offer them a fixed number of new shares for every share they currently hold. The shares will normally be priced below the current market price of existing shares. If you buy all the shares offered your overall holding in the company will remain the same.

Rounding Charge

An adjustment upwards of the price of units in a trust to

avoid unwieldy fractions. Managers of authorised unit trusts must limit this rounding up to 1.25p or 1%, whichever is less.

RPI
The Retail Prices Index measures the cost of living. Key constituents include the mortgage rate, price of petrol and food.

S

Scrip Issue
A free issue of new shares to current shareholders in direct proportion to their existing holdings. Often used by a company when the existing shares have become so expensive that they are difficult to market.

Securities
The general term for stocks and shares.

Settlement Day
The day when share buyers have to pay for their purchases. Also known as account day. It is usually the Monday, ten days after the end of the account.

Share Certificate
Document confirming ownership of the shares. The certificate is issued by the company's registrars, and usually arrives some three weeks after you have bought the shares.

Share Exchange
Most unit trust groups run schemes under which they swop shares for units in a unit trust. Details of individual schemes vary and many groups will only accept blue chip shares or shares in companies where they already invest. Such swops count as disposal for the purposes of assessing capital gains tax liability, so the potential tax bill should be taken into account before opting for such a scheme.

Short

Going 'short' is the phrase used to describe the action of someone who thinks the price of a share is going to fall and hopes to make a quick profit. At the start of the account he will sell shares he does not own and hope that before he has to deliver the stock, he will get the chance to buy the shares at a lower price. If the price of the shares does fall, he will make an instant profit. If they rise he will have to buy the shares at the higher price and will therefore incur an instant loss.

Shorts

Gilts which are due to be repaid within five years.

SIB

Securities and Investment Board. Set up in 1985 under the chairmanship of Kenneth Berrill, KCB. Provided the white paper on Financial Services in the UK becomes law, it will be the self-regulating body for the investment industry.

Spread

The difference between the buying and selling price of shares or unit trusts.

Stag

Someone who buys shares in a new issue with the intention of selling them straight away for a quick profit.

Stamp Duty

A tax payable on the purchase of ordinary shares, preference shares and convertible loan stock. At the moment it is 1% of the value of the purchase. There is no stamp duty on gilts, allotment letters or loan stock.

Stock

A general term used interchangeably with shares or securities. Specifically, it is used in relation to fixed interest securities with a face value of £100.

Stock Exchange

A non-profit making organisation owned by its members which supervises and run the market in securities. It has four main functions: 1) to supply the technical and administrative services necessary for the swift and efficient transaction of members business; 2) to uphold minimum entry requirements and maintain standards of competence and integrity among its members; 3) through stringent listing rules, to establish quality control over companies seeking and maintaining a quotation; and, 4) as a trade association, to represent both the interests of its members and users of its services.

Stock Exchange Council

The governing body of the Stock Exchange. It consists of 52 people. Forty-six are elected by the members, five are lay members and the final chair is reserved for the government broker. Although there are no formal proposals to change its composition it is likely that in future the number of serving members will be decreased to more manageable proportions.

Stock Exchange Member

Someone who has passed the Stock Exchange exams, been elected and has abided by the exchange's rules of conduct.

Stockbroker

One of two specialist members of the Stock Exchange. A broker acts as agent and adviser to the public who wish to buy and sell securities. Brokers are not paid directly for their services but earn commission based on the size and type of transaction concluded.

Stockjobber

Acts as a principal, buying and selling shares for his own account. Makes a market in shares and transacts business with stockbrokers. Jobbers earn their living by selling shares for more than they cost. The amount they earn is related to both overall turnover and their skill at judging individual price movements.

Suspension

The main reason a share is suspended is to avoid a false market in the shares. In the majority of cases the company itself, usually prompted by its advisers, will ask the Exchange to suspend its shares temporarily until the price sensitive information can be clarified and made freely available to all.

Subdivision of Units

If the price of a unit trust increases to an unwieldy level, the managers may decide to subdivide the units. This does not alter the actual value of a unit holder's investment but simply the number of units held.

Subscription Day

The day on which unit trusts or offshore funds which do not alter their prices daily are prepared to buy and sell units.

Switching Discount

A discount given to existing investors when they switch their money between unit trusts run by a single group. At the moment it varies in size from 1–5%.

Take-over

When one company buys another. Once a single individual holds 30% of a quoted company under the current rules he is required to make a full bid for the company.

Take-over Panel

Supervises the conduct of potential purchasers of quoted companies. It has a strict code of conduct which covers the activities of both the bidding company and the directors of the target company.

Talisman

Transfer Accounting, Lodging for Investors and Stock Management for Jobbers. The term used for the Stock

118

Exchange's computerised settlement system.

Tap
Most commonly used in the phrase 'tap stock' to describe a supply of gilts which the government broker will sell at a given price. It can also be used when there is a steady stream of sellers of a certain share.

Tax Credit
When you receive dividends from your shares or distributions from a unit trust you will also be sent a tax credit to show that 30% tax has been paid on your behalf. If you do not pay income tax, you can reclaim the amount paid. Higher rate taxpayers will have a further income tax bill.

Tender   *TESSAS Tax Exempt Special Savings Accounts.*
A rather unpopular method of setting the price for new issues and shares. Potential investors are asked to name their own price provided it is higher than a stated minimum. It is very difficult for private investors to judge the appropriate price and to be nifty enough not to get caught by the changes in institutional sentiment.

Traded Option
An option that is quoted in the traded option market run by the Stock Exchange. It can be bought and sold through a stockbroker.

Transfer Deed
If you wish to sell your shares then you must sign a transfer deed. This only applies to registered stock and enables the company register to be kept up to date.

True and Fair
The phrase used by accountants to describe the report and accounts of a company which conforms to the rules laid down by the Companies Act.

Trust
A group of people or institution which looks after the invest-

ments of another. Under the law of trusts there are strict regulations governing their behaviour and the way they carry out their obligations.

Trust Deed
In the case of unit trusts the deed is a legal document between the trustees and fund managers which lays down the framework within which managers must operate.

Trustees
Institutions such as banks or insurance companies which are both independent of the fund managers and of proven integrity. Their role is to ensure that the managers keep to the rules laid down in the trust deed and where necessary to defend unit holders' interests. Their fees are paid by the managers out of the management charges.

U

USM
Unlisted Securities Market. This is the junior version of the stock market designed for companies who wish to have their shares available to the public in a regulated way but do not qualify for a full listing. In particular it enables relatively young companies where the owners do not wish to lose control of the business to tap public money.

Unconditional
A bid goes unconditional when the potential predator's terms have been accepted by more than 50% of the target company's shareholders. Once a bid has gone unconditional the bidder is required to take up the shares offered to him at the terms he offered, even if he does not gain full control.

Underwriter
Normally a merchant bank, broker or trust who agrees for a fee to buy shares in a new issue in the event of those shares

not being sold to the public. This provides the company issuing the new shares with a safety net and the security of knowing that the fresh money will be raised.

Unfranked Income

Income which in the hands of a unit trust becomes subject to corporation tax. Trusts which only invest in gilts, local authority and fixed interest stock are required to pay basic rate income tax rather than the higher rate of corporation tax.

Unit Trust

A fund authorised by the Department of Trade. Its main aim is to invest in equities and there are strict rules governing its other investment activities. The trust is owned by unit holders and the price of their units are directly related in an agreed formula to the value of the trusts' shares. The number of units is increased or decreased to reflect the flow of money in and out of the fund. The units are priced in such a way that the value of each unit in relation to the fund is unchanged. Unit trusts can be freely marketed in the UK and they do not pay capital gains tax on their internal share dealing.

Unit Trust Association

It is partly a self-regulatory body set up by the unit trust industry. It lobbies on the industry's behalf to government and runs an information service for customers. Unit Trust Association members manage 96% of the money in unit trusts.

Unit Allocation

When you buy an insurance policy which is linked to a fund not all your money is invested in units. The unit allocation will determine how much of your money is placed in the fund and how much goes to cover the insurance element and marketing expenses.

Unit Trust Instrument Duty

A rather archaic tax of ¼% of new money added to the trust.

It is payable by the managers to the taxman and is included in the difference between the buying and selling costs of units.

Unitisation
The conversion of an investment trust into a unit trust. The costs of such an operation is usually equivalent to about 6% of the investment trust's assets so it is only worth doing if the price of the shares in the investment trust are substantially lower than the net assets per share.

Unlisted Investment
These are shares in companies which are not quoted on a recognised stock exchange. They tend to be difficult to trade and equally problematic to value.

W

Warrants
A certificate giving the registered holder the right to buy shares at a fixed price some time in the future. They are traded on the stock exchange and their price tends to be more volatile than the company's shares.

Withdrawal Scheme
A system under which steady income can be obtained from a unit trust investment. This is achieved by the sale of units. This may be more tax efficient than going for a high income unit trust but it can result in a decline in the real value of your capital very quickly if the trust's overall performance lags the rise in retail prices.

Withholding Tax
This is a tax which is levied by most foreign governments on dividends paid out by their native companies to residents outside its jurisdiction. Investors can usually reclaim this tax.

X

XD
Ex dividend. Shares which do not qualify for dividends.

XR
Ex-rights. Shares which do not qualify for rights issue.

XS
Ex-scrip. Shares which do not qualify for scrip issue.

Y

Yearling
A local authority stock which matures in one year. Often used as a benchmark for interest rate trends.

Yield
The return on a security based on its current price and current gross interest or dividend.

Yield Gap
The difference between the yield on a 15 year gilt and on ordinary shares.

Z

Zero Coupon Bond
A bond which pays no interest over its life but which is issued well below par. They are very popular in the US as investors are guaranteed a large capital gain. Due to unfavourable tax treatment in the UK they are not widely used here.

Section III

Addresses of Companies and Firms which are Stock Exchange Members

Firms and Companies

B or **J** following the name of a firm or company denotes that it is carrying on business as a broker or a jobber.

AITKEN CAMPBELL & CO (J)
69 St Georges Place, Glasgow G2 1JN
Telephone: 041-248 6966 (Office); 041-221 3902/3 (Dealers)
Stx: 226. Stx (Dealers): 227/228/229/230
Partners: Four

AKROYD & SMITHERS PLC (J)
Limited Corporate Member
. Austin Friars House, 2-6 Austin Friars, London EC2N 2EE
Telephone: 01-588 4535. Stx: 4664
Telegrams: Retinoid London EC2
Directors: Eight

ANDERSON & CO (B)
62 London Wall, London EC2R 7DQ
Telephone: 01-638 1200. Stx: 7191
Telegrams: Cinnamon London EC3. Telex: 885263
Partners: Seven

A. C. ANDERSON & CO (B)
49 Bath Street, Glasgow G2 2DL
Telephone: 041-221 2048/9
Partners: Three

S. P. ANGEL & CO (B)
Moorgate Hall, 155-157 Moorgate, London EC2M 6XB

Telephone: 01-588 3427. Stx: 4408
Telegrams: Angelico Stock London. Telex: 8955762
Partners: Four

ARNOLD STANSBY & CO (B)
Dennis House, Marsden Street, Manchester M2 3JJ
Telephone: 061-832 8554. Stx: 260
Partners: Two

ASHTON TOD McLAREN (B)
13 Castle Street, Liverpool L2 4SU
Telephone: 051-236 8281. Stx (Dealers): 271
Other Offices:
Ashton Tod McLaren
Friarsgate, Warrington, Cheshire WA1 2RS
Telephone: (0925) 572671
Ashton Tod McLaren
16 Watergate Row, Chester CH1 2LD
Telephone: (0244) 310228
Partners: Five

ASHWORTH SONS & BARRATT (B)
26 Pall Mall, Manchester M2 1JS
Telephone: 061-832 4812
Stx: 261. Stx (Dealers): 262
Other Offices:
2 Quennevais Precinct, St Brelade, Jersey, Channel Islands
Telephone: (0534) 44191/2
1st Floor, 7 Le Pollet, St Peter Port, Guernsey, Channel Islands
Telephone: (0481) 20152
Partners: Five

ASTAIRE & CO LD (B)
Limited Corporate Member
117 Bishopsgate, London EC2
Telephone: 01-283 2081. Stx: 2461
Telegrams: Astco London. Telex: 883168
Other Offices:
Astaire & Co Far East
901 Hutchison House, Hong Kong
Telephone: 5 264081/2/3
Telegrams: Astaire Hong Kong. Telex: HX 74330
Astaire & Co LD
90a George Street, Edinburgh EH2 3DF
Directors: Seven

BARRATT & COOKE (B)
5 Opie Street, Norwich, Norfolk NR1 3DW
Telephone: (0603) 24236
Other Offices:
Warnford Court, 1st Floor Rooms 99/100/101
Throgmorton Street, London EC2N 2AT
Telephone: 01-638 0159
Midland Bank Chambers, Mansfield, Nottingham NG18 1JD
Telephone: (0623) 23596
Partners: Three

BATTYE, WIMPENNY & DAWSON (B)
11 Station Street, Huddersfield HD1 1LX
Telephone: (0484) 21718/30555/21826
Telegrams: Moorcock Huddersfield
Partners: Two

BEALE SHEFFIELD & CO (B)
Unlimited Corporate Member
15 South Mall, Cork
Telephone: Cork (021) 20828/9/30, 20326
Telex: E1 26194
Shareholders: Two

BEKHOR (A.J.) & CO (B)
Unlimited Corporate Member
Migdal House, 12a Finsbury Square, London EC2A 1LT
Telephone: 01-628 6050. Stx: 2464
Telegrams: RAYBEK Stock London. Telex: 886182
Other Offices:
Bekhor (A.J.) & Co
2 Queens Gate, 1 Osborne Road
Southsea, Portsmouth PO5 3LX
Telephone: (0705) 21766
Bekhor (A.J.) & Co
3 Library Ramp, Gibraltar
Telephone: 74577
Bekhor (A.J.) & Co
7 College Street, Nottingham NG1 5AQ
Telephone: (0602) 414344
Bekhor (A.J.) & Co
3 Devonshire Square, Bexhill-on-Sea, Sussex TN40 1AJ
Telephone: (0424) 219111
Bekhor (A.J.) & Co
98 High Street, Lymington, Hants.
Telephone: (0590) 74288
Bekhor (A.J.) & Co
153 High Street, Poole, Dorset
Telephone: (0202) 678081
Bekhor (A.J.) & Co
PO Box 506, Fountain House, 81 Fountain Street, Manchester M2 2EE
Telephone: 061-832 6644/061-228 2666. Stx: 284/235
Bekhor (A.J.) & Co
9 Great Stuart Street, Edinburgh
Bekhor (A.J.) & Co
32 St Nicholas Street, Bristol 1
Bekhor (A.J.) & Co
31 Watling Street, Canterbury, Kent
Telephone: (0227) 56085
Bekhor (A.J.) & Co
City Wall House, 18-22 Chiswell Street, London EC2Y 9AY
Bekhor (A.J.) & Co
1-3 College Hill, London EC4R 2RA
Telephone: 01-236 0262/01-628 6050. Stx: 3200/4385
Bakhor (A.J.) & Co
Provincial House, 1 Strand, Torquay TQ1 2RH
Telephone: (0803) 273337

Bakhor (A.J.) & Co
38 Gay Street, Bath, Avon
Shareholders: Seven
Limited Partner: One

BELL HOULDSWORTH & CO (B)
PO Box 329, 4 Norfolk Street, Manchester M60 2QL
Telephone: 061-834 3542/061-832 8671
Stx: 264. Stx (Dealers): 263
Partners: Three

BELL, LAWRIE, MACGREGOR & CO (B)
PO Box 8, Erskine House, 68-73 Queen Street, Edinburgh EH2 4AE
Telephone: 031-225 2566
Stx (Dealers): 231/240 Glasgow Code
Telex: 72260
Other Office:
52 Buccleuch Street, Dumfries DG1 2AH
Telephone: (0387) 52361/2
Partners: Fourteen

BISGOOD BISHOP & CO LD (J)
Limited Corporate Member
Copthall House, 48 Copthall Avenue, London EC2R 7DN
Telephone: 01-628 3033. Stx: 4866
Directors: Eight
Special Directors: Four
Associated Members with personal liability: Six

BLANKSTONE SINGTON & CO (B)
Martins Building, 6 Water Street, Liverpool L2 3SP
Telephone: 051-227 1881
Stx: 252. Stx (Dealers): 273
Partners: Four

BLOXHAM TOOLE O'DONNELL (B)
Curran House, 11 Fleet Street, Dublin 2
Telephone: Dublin 776653
Telegrams: Bloxham Dublin. Telex: 25199
Partners: Three

BRANSTON & GOTHARD (B)
61 Cheapside, London EC2V 6BD
Telephone: 01-236 4347. Stx: 2418
Telegrams: Estranged London
Partners: Four

BREARLEY (JAMES) & SONS (B)
31 King Street, Blackpool FY1 3DQ
Telephone: (0253) 21474
Stx: 276 (Liverpool Code)
Partners: Three

BREWIN DOLPHIN & CO (B)
5 Giltspur Street, London EC1A 9DE
Telephone: 01-248 4400. Stx: 2393/2394/2395
Telegrams: Zenos London. Telex: 21423
Other Office:
Caversham House, 19 Queen Street

St Helier, Jersey, Channel Islands
Telephone: (0534) 27391
Partners: Twelve

BROADBRIDGE LAWSON & CO (B)
16 Park Place, Leeds LS1 2SJ
Telephone: (0532) 443721 (5 lines) 443726/7 (Dealers)
Other Offices:
19 King Street, Wakefield WF1 2SP
Telephone: (0924) 372601/371594
Fountain Chambers, Fountain Street, Halifax HX1 1LS
Telephone: (0422) 67707/67708
Partners: Five

BUCKMASTER & MOORE (B)
18th & 19th Floors, The Stock Exchange, London EC2P 2JT
Telephone: 01-588 2868. Stx: 3003
Telegrams: Buckmore London Telex. Telex: 883229
Other Offices:
Brompton House, 3 Athol Street, Douglas, Isle of Man
Telephone: (0624) 27134
88 Lincoln Road, Peterborough PE1 1SN
Telephone: (0733) 311611
Partners: Thirty-one
Limited Partner(s): Two

BUTLER & BRISCOE (B)
3 College Green, Dublin 2
Telephone: Dublin 777348
Telegrams: Alert Dublin. Telex: 52820
Other Office:
7 Lower Rowe Street, Wexford
Telephone: Wexford 22187
Partners: Six

CAMPBELL NEILL & CO (B)
69 St Georges Place, Glasgow G2 1JN
Telephone: 041-248 6271 (10 lines)
Stx: 232/234. Stx (Dealers): 233
Telegrams: Investment Glasgow
Other Office:
City Gate House, 5th Floor
39-45 Finsbury Square, London EC2A 1PX
Telephone: 01-920 9661/2. Stx (Dealers): 7469
Partners: Eight

CAMPBELL O'CONNOR & CO (B)
8 Cope Street, Dublin 2
Telephone: Dublin 771773/771834
Telex: 25633
Partners: Two

CAPEL-CURE MYERS (B)
Bath House, Holborn Viaduct, London EC1A 2EU
Telephone: 01-236 5080. Stx: 4621
Telegrams: Procur London EC1A 2EU. Telex: 886653
Stock Deliveries:
Room 1, First Floor

49 Queen Victoria Street, London EC4N
Other Office:
9 Hope Street, Edinburgh EH2 4EL
Telephone: 031-225 2171. Stx: 237
Telegrams: Procur Edinburgh. Telex: 727265
Partners: Thirty-nine
Limited Partner: One

CAPEL (JAMES) & CO (B)
Unlimited Corporate Member
Winchester House, 100 Old Broad Street, London EC2N 1BQ
Telephone: 01-588 6010. Stx: 7201
Telegrams: Capels London EC2. Telex: 888866
Other Offices:
James Capel & Co
3 Mulcaster Street, St Helier, Jersey, Channel Islands
Telephone: (0534) 37428/9
James Capel International SA
103 Grand Rue, Luxembourg
Telephone: 46-85-11
James Capel (Far East) LD
Room 2001, Hutchison House, 10 Harcourt Road, Hong Kong
Telephone: 5-237156
James Capel (Far East) LD
4 Raffles Quay 05-00, Finlayson House, Singapore 0104
Telephone: 2248677/2248683
James Capel (USA) LD
3 Mulcaster Street, St Helier, Jersey, Channel Islands
Telephone: (0534) 37428/9
James Capel & Co
8th Floor, Nippon Press Center Building
2-2-1 Uchisaiwaicho, Chiyoda-ku, Tokyo 100, Japan
Telephone: 593-2091
Shareholders: 62

CARR, WORKMAN, PATTERSON, TOPPING & CO (B)
Prudential Building, Fountain Street, Belfast BT1 5EY
Telephone: Belfast 245044 (5 lines)
Stx: 278 (Liverpool Code)
Telegrams: Investor Belfast
Partners: Three

CARSWELL & CO (B)
69 St Georges Place, Glasgow G2 1BU
Telephone: 041-221 3402. Stx: 235
Telegrams: Transfer Glasgow
Partners: Three

CAVE & SONS (B)
9-11 Hazelwood Road, Northampton
Telephone: (0604) 21421
Telegrams: Cavansons Northampton
Partners: Three

CAWOOD SMITHIE & CO (B)
22 East Parade, Harrogate, North Yorkshire HG1 5LT
Telephone: (0423) 66781/522226
Other Offices:

73 Church Street, Hartlepool, Cleveland TS24 7DN
Telephone: (0429) 72231/2, 74491/2
48a High Street, Stokesley, Middlesbrough, Cleveland TS9 5AX
Telephone: (0642) 712771
11 Harley Street, London W1N 1DA
Partners: Five

CAZENOVE & CO (B)
12 Tokenhouse Yard, London EC2R 7AN
Telephone: 01-588 2828. Stx: 7301
Telegrams: Cazenove London EC2. Telex: 886758, 886798
Other Offices:
Cazenove Australia Pty Limited
Level 42, Australia Square, Sydney 2000, Australia
Telephone: 010 612 233 4022
Cazenove & Co
5th Floor, French House, 54 Marshall Street, Johannesburg, South Africa
Telephone: 010 2711 834 5538
Cazenove Financiere
& Geneva Branch Office
2 Rue Bartholoni, Geneva, Switzerland
Telephone: 010 4122 203 511. Telex: 427480
Cazenove & Co (Overseas)
808 Hutchison House, Hong Kong
Telephone: 010 8525 264 211. Telex: 74355
Cazenove & Co (Overseas)
3F Nanbu Building, 3-3 Kioi-Cho, Chiyoda-ku, Tokyo, Japan
Telephone: 010 813 263 1706
Cazenove Inc
400 Montgomery Street, Suite 501, San Francisco, California, USA 94104
Telephone: 0101 415 392 0447
Cazenove Inc
67 Wall Street, New York City, New York 10005, USA
Telephone: 0101 212 747 1225
Cazenove Inc
12 Tokenhouse Yard, London EC2R 7AN
Telephone: 01-588 2828
Partners: Thirty-seven

CHALMERS OGILVIE & CO (B)
10 Panmure Street, Dundee DD1 9BA
Telephone: (0382) 26282
Partners: Three

CHAMBERS & REMINGTON (B)
Canterbury House, 85 Newhall Street, Birmingham B3 1LS
Telephone: 021-236 2577. Stx: 263/264
Stx (Dealers): (London) 7689/7680
Partners: Three

WILLIAM CHAPMAN, TREASE & CO (B)
Norwich Union House, South Parade, Nottingham NG1 2LN
Telephone: (0602) 476772. Telex: 377332
Partners: Six

CHARLESWORTH & CO (J)
Warnford Court, London EC2
Telephone: 01-588 3758; 01-606 4560/1672

Stx: 5024 7692 2191 2192/3609
Stx (Dealers): 3631 3632 3641 3642
Partners: Four

CHARLTON BRETT & BOUGHEY (B)
367 Lord Street, Southport PR8 1NS
Telephone: (0704) 32282. Telex: 67500
Other Office:
PO Box 1, 5 Grimshaw Street, Burnley, Lancashire BB11 2AX
Telephone: (0282) 22042
Partners: Three

CHARLTON SEAL DIMMOCK & CO (B)
76 Cross Street, Manchester M60 2EP
Telephone: 061-832 3488
Stx: 265 266. Stx (Dealers): 224
Other Office:
City Gate House, 5th Floor, 39-45 Finsbury Square, London EC2A 1PX
Telephone: 01-588 2686. Stx: 3471 3472 3473
Partners: Six

CHARLTON SEAL (B)
Unlimited Corporate Member
Stock Exchange Trading Subsidiary of Charlton Seal Dimmock & Co
Channel House, Green Street, St Helier, Jersey, Channel Islands
Telephone: (0534) 25225/6
Directors: Two

COATES (WM.F.) & CO (B)
Northern Bank House, 8-9 Donegall Square North, Belfast BT1 5LX
Telephone: Belfast 223456 (10 lines). Telegrams: Alpha Belfast
Partners: Four

COBBOLD (A.H.) & CO (B)
61 Devonshire Road, Southampton, Hampshire SO9 1XL
Telephone: (0703) 333292/4. Telex: 477823 Bold G
Other Offices:
Warnford Court, Throgmorton Street, London EC2N 2AT
Telephone: 01-920 9441
3 St Peter Street, Winchester, Hampshire SO23 8BJ
Telephone: (0962) 52362
Partners: Seven

COLEMAN (R.A.) & CO (B)
204 High Street, Bangor, Gwynedd LL57 1NY
Telephone: (0248) 353242. Stx: 4307
Partners: Four
Limited Partner: One

COLLINS (E.J.) & CO (B)
Friars House, 39-41 New Broad Street, London EC2M 1NH
Telephone: 01-588 7666. Stx: 2408
Telegrams: Collcoop London EC2
Partners: Three

CONI GILBERT & SANKEY (B)
10 Throgmorton Avenue, Throgmorton Street, London EC2N 2DH
Telephone: 01-638 8871. Stx: 3557/3558
Telegrams: 10 Throgmorton Avenue. Telex: 8813643
Other Office:

60 Waterloo Road, Wolverhampton WV1 4QW
Telephone: (0902) 28711
Partners: Eight

COOKE (HENRY) LUMSDEN & CO (B)
Unlimited Corporate Member
PO Box 369, Arkwright House, Parsonage Gardens, Manchester M60 3AH
Telephone: 061-834 2332. Stx: 267/268
Telex: 667783
Other Office:
City Wall House, 84-90 Chiswell Street, London EC1Y 4TX
Telephone: 01-628 0411. Stx: 3561/3562/3563/3564
Telegrams: Lumsden London EC4. Telex: 888417
Shareholders: Seventeen

COOMBS (T.C.) & CO (B)
Unlimited Corporate Member
5-7 Ireland Yard, London EC4V 5EE
Telephone: 01-248 2033
Fax No: 01-236 9184. Stx: 4788
Telex: 8811413 TOPCAT G
Other Offices:
T. C. Coombs (Overseas) LD
44th Floor, Hopewell Centre, Hong Kong
Telephone: 5 237 012
T. C. Coombs (Australia) Pty LD
7th Floor, 351 Collins Street, Melbourne, Victoria 3000, Australia
Telephone: 010 613 614 1856
Coombs (T.C.) & Co
5 York Road, Tunbridge Wells, Kent TN1 1JK
Telephone: (0892) 39501
Shareholders: Four

CROOKALL (RAMSEY) & CO (B)
25 Athol Street, Douglas, Isle of Man
Telephone: (0624) 3171/4, 23884/5
Telex: 627530
Partners: Two

CUNNINGHAM (JOSIAS) & CO (B)
2 Bridge Street, Belfast BT1 1NX
Telephone: Belfast 246005
Partners: Six

DAFFERN & STEPHENSON (B)
66 Queens Road, Coventry CV1 3FU
Telephone: (0203) 25352. Telegrams: Daffern
Partners: Two

DARBISHIRE MALCOMSON & COATES (B)
4th Floor, 13 Donegall Place, Belfast BT1 5NT
Telephone: Belfast 231617
Partners: Two

DAVY (J. & E.) (B)
63 Dawson Street, Dublin 2
Telephone: Dublin 772416
Telegrams: Exact Dublin. Telex: 25865
Partners: Nine

DE ZOETE & BEVAN (B)
25 Finsbury Circus, London EC2M 7EE
Telephone: 01-588 4141. Stx: 2511/4597
Telegrams: Zanton London EC2M 7EE
Telex: 888221, 883179, 8812750
Other Office:
De Zoete & Bevan (Far East)
81a New Henry House, 10 Ice House Street, Hong Kong
Telephone: 010-852-5-248136. Telex: HX 62442
Partners: Forty-four

DILLON & WALDRON (B)
10 Anglesea Street, Dublin 2
Telephone: Dublin 777809
Telegrams: Waldron Telex Dublin
Telex: 5765
Partners: Three

DOAK & CO (B)
1st Floor, Ulster Bank Building, 3-5 Suffolk Street, Dublin 2
Telephone: Dublin 770952 (4 lines)
Partners: Two

DOUGLAS (JOHN M.) & EYKYN BROS (B)
30 College Street, London EC4R 2TE
Telephone: 01-248 4277. Stx: 4261/4285
Telegrams: Eykyn London EC2
Partners: Three

DUDGEON (B)
Unlimited Corporate Member
25 Suffolk Street, Dublin 2
Telephone: Dublin 777314
Telegrams: Dudgeon Dublin
Telex: 25299
Shareholders: Four

DUNKLEY MARSHALL (B)
4 London Wall Buildings, London EC2M 5NX
Telephone: 01-638 1282. Stx: 4265
Telegrams: Solidarity London EC2. Telex: 883787
Other Office:
3 Poole Road, Bournemouth, Dorset
Partners: Fourteen

EARNSHAW HAES & SONS (B)
17 Tokenhouse Yard, London EC2R 7LB
Telephone: 01-588 5699. Stx: 3016
Telex: London 886202
Partners: Nine
Limited Partner: One

EDWARDS JONES & WILCOX (J)
Stock Exchange Buildings, 33 Great Charles Street
Queensway, Birmingham B3 3JJ
Telephone: 021-236 6117 (office); 021-236 6112 (market)
Stx (Dealers): 231/241
Partners: Three

ELIOTT (GILBERT) & CO (B)
381-399 Salisbury House, London Wall, London EC2M 5SB
Telephone: 01-628 6782. Stx: 4899
Telegrams: Gibeliott London EC2. Telex: 888886
Partners: Seventeen

FARLEY & THOMPSON (B)
Pine Grange, Bath Road, Bournemouth BH1 2NU
Telephone: (0202) 26277. Telegrams: Investment
Partners: Two

FERNYHOUGH & CO (B)
Lloyds Bank Buildings, 33 Cross Street, Manchester M2 4LP
Telephone: 061-833 0961. Stx: 270
Telegrams: Ferny Manchester
Partners: Two

FIELDING NEWSON-SMITH & CO (B)
Garrard House, 31 Gresham Street, London EC2V 7DX
Telephone: 01-606 7711. Stx: 4011
Telegrams: FNS LDN. Telex: 883395
Partners: Thirty-eight

FINN (J.M.) & CO (B)
Salisbury House, London Wall, London EC2M 5TA
Telephone: 01-628 9688. Stx: 4488
Telegrams: Jayemfinn London Telex
Telex: 887281
Partners: Fourteen

FISKE & CO (B)
Salisbury House, London Wall, London EC2M 5QS
Telephone: 01-638 4681. Stx: 7744
Telex: 897482
Partners: Six

FOSTER & BRAITHWAITE (B)
22 Austin Friars, London EC2N 2BU
Telephone: 01-588 6111
Stx: 2501/2502/2503/2504
Telex: 8954140
Partners: Five

FYSHE HORTON FINNEY & CO (B)
Devonshire House, 40-42 Great Charles Street
Queensway, Birmingham B3 2NE
Telephone: 021-236 3111/7586
Stx: 261/253
Partners: Four
Limited Partner: One

GALL & EKE (B)
Charlotte House, 10 Charlotte Street, Manchester M1 4FL
Telephone: 061-228 2511. Stx: 271
Telegrams: Galleon Manchester/Winder Manchester
Partners: Two

GALLOWAY & PEARSON (B)
Warnford Court, Throgmorton Street, London EC2N 2AU

Telephone: 01-628 8211. Stx: 4551
Telegrams: Gallus London Telex
Telex: 885384/8956819
Partners: Twelve

GARRATT (HENRY J.) & CO (B)
Bourne House, 34 Copthall Avenue, London EC2
Telephone: 01-628 9545. Stx: 4557
Telegrams: Embarked London EC2
Other Offices:
67 Hamlet Court Road, Westcliff-on-Sea, Essex SS0 7EU
Telephone: (0702) 347173/347178
Broadwalk House, Southernhay, Exeter, South Devon
Telephone: (0392) 52679
Partners: Four

GILBERT JEFFS & CO (B)
Grosvenor House, 14 Bennetts Hill, Birmingham B2 5SE
Telephone: 021-643 7861/4; 7507/500
Stx (Dealers): 268/274
Partners: Three

GILBEY (SOUTHARD) McNISH & CO (B)
Leadenhall Buildings, 1 Leadenhall Street, London EC3V 1NH
Telephone: 01-623 7466. Stx: 2091
Telegrams: Tupto London EC3
Partners: Two

GILES (A.B.) & CRESSWELL (J)
Pinners Hall, Austin Friars, London EC2 2HE
Telephone: 01-628 3475/6. Stx: 3044/3045
Partners: Six

GILES & OVERBURY (B)
Diana House, 33 Chiswell Street, London EC1Y 4ES
Telephone: 01-638 4690 (office); 01-638 4698/9 (dealers)
Stx: 2519. Stx (Dealers): 7691/5291/5230
Telegrams: Gossamer London EC2
Telex: MARGIE-G 965536
Partners: Two

GODFRAY, DERBY & CO (B)
Broad Street House, Broad Street, Wells, Somerset BA5 1DJ
Telephone: (0749) 76373
Other Offices:
6 Broad Street Place, London EC2
Telephone: 01-638 0767/01-638 4486 (Partners/Dealers)
Stx: 4485
1 Northumberland Buildings, Queen Square, Bath BA1 2JB
Telephone: (0225) 65811
Partners: Three

GOODBODY & WILKINSON (B)
Unlimited Corporate Member
1 Crow Street, Dublin 2
Telephone: Dublin 773481/777528
Telegrams: Goodbody Dublin
Telex: 25104 GBDY E1
Other Offices:

Warnford Court, 1st Floor Rooms 99/100/101
Throgmorton Street, London EC2N 2AT
Telephone: 01-628 4131/2. Stx: 7945
87 South Mall, Cork
Shareholders: Five

GORDON (PANMURE) & CO (B)
9 Moorfields Highwalk, London EC2Y 9DS
Telephone: 01-638 4010. Stx: 2095/2096/2097
Telegrams: Panmure London EC2. Telex: 883832/883833
Partners: Twenty-six

GREENE & CO (B)
Bilbao House, 36-38 New Broad Street, London EC2M 1NU
Telephone: 01-628 7241. Stx: 2151
Telegrams: Greenstok London EC2. Telex: 8955502 GREENE G
Partners: Eight

GREENWELL (W.) & CO (B)
Bow Bells House, Bread Street, London EC4M 9EL
Telephone: 01-236 2040. Stx: 3077
Telegrams: Greenwells London EC4. Telex: 883006
Other Office:
W. Greenwell Inc.
450 Park Avenue, New York, NY 10022, USA
Telephone: 212 832 7428
Partners: Forty-two
Limited Partner: One

GRIEG, MIDDLETON & CO (B)
78 Old Broad Street, London EC2M 1JE
Telephone: 01-920 0481. Stx: 3227
Telex: 887296
Other Offices:
139 St Vincent Street, Glasgow G2 5JP
Telephone: 041-221 8103. Stx: 262
Telex: 776695
Court House, Tailor's Court, Broad Street, Bristol BS1 2EX
Telephone: (0272) 24013
Partners: Seventeen

GRENFELL AND COLEGRAVE (B)
55-61 Moorgate, London EC2R 6DR
Telephone: 01-628 6044. Stx: 2154
Telegrams: Grenco. Telex: 28902
Partners: Twenty-seven

GRIEVESON GRANT & CO (B)
59 Gresham Street, London EC2P 2DS
Telephone: 01-606 4433. Stx: 2733
Telegrams: Grieveson London Telex
Telex: 887336/887337/887338
Other Offices:
Grieveson Grant & Co
Union House, Eridge Road, Tunbridge Wells, Kent
Grieveson Grant International LD
Suite 1109, 11 Beacon Street, Boston, Massachussetts, USA 02108
Telephone: (617) 523 5455. Telex: 92-1730

Grieveson Grant International LD
PO Box 119, Commerce House, Les Banques
St Peter Port, Guernsey, Channel Islands
Grieveson Grant & Co
Shin Kudan Building, Kudan Minami 2-2-4, Chiyoda-Ku, Tokyo 102, Japan
Telephone: (03) 230 1436/1506. Telex: 02324986
Partners: Sixty-five

GRIFFITHS & LAMB (B)
York House, 38 Great Charles Street, Queensway, Birmingham B3 3JY
Telephone: 021-236 6641
Stx (Dealers): 270
Partners: Five

HALL GRAHAM BRADFORD (B)
Bilbao House, 36-38 New Broad Street, London EC2M 1NU
Telephone: 01-628 7961/2/3/4
Stx: 3391/3392. Stx (Dealers): 2486
Telegrams: Passim London EC2
Partners: Three

HANSON & CO (B)
6 Regent Terrace, South Parade, Doncaster, South Yorkshire DN1 2EL
Telephone: (0302) 23223
Other Offices:
4 Lendal, York YO1 2AD
Telephone: (0904) 22085
Pendle House, 73 Preston New Road, Blackburn, Lancashire BB2 6BA
Telephone: (0254) 59611
The Chambers, 53 Guildhall Street, Preston PR1 3NU
Telephone: (0772) 556248
National Westminster Bank Buildings, 66 Church Street, Lancaster LA1 1LW
Telephone: (0524) 32582
Churchgate House, Churchgate, Bolton BL1 1HL
Telephone: (0204) 24232
Partners: Eleven

HARGREAVE (MARSDEN W.) HALE & CO (B)
8-10 Springfield Road, Blackpool FY1 1QN
Telephone: (0253) 21575
Other Offices:
Williams and Glyn's Bank Chambers, St Annes
Lytham St Annes, Lancashire FY8 1RW
Telephone: (0253) 722166
7 Moor Park Avenue, Preston PR1 6AS
Telephone: (0772) 21948
Partners: Six

HARRIS, ALLDAY, LEA & BROOKS (B)
Stock Exchange Buildings, 33 Great Charles Street
Queensway, Birmingham B3 3JN
Telephone: 021-233 1222
Stx: 259. Stx (Dealers): 232/251/252
Other Offices:
Elgin House, 11 West Bar, Banbury, Oxon OX16 9SD
Telephone: (0295) 2103
2 St Leonards Close, Bridgnorth, Shropshire

Telephone: (07462) 61444
Partners: Eight

HENDERSON CROSTHWAITE & CO (B)
194-200 Bishopsgate, London EC2
Telephone: 01-283 8577
Stx: 2331. Stx (Dealers): 4091
Telegrams: Hendercros Telex LDN
Telex: 883924/8956765
Other Offices:
Henderson Crosthwaite & Co
Virginia House, The Butts, Worcester WR1 3PL
Telephone: (0905) 29551
Henderson Crosthwaite & Co
Thorpe House, 27 King Street, Hereford HR4 9BX
Telephone: (0432) 265647
Henderson Crosthwaite & Co
25 Imperial Square, Cheltenham GL50 1QZ
Telephone: (0242) 514756
Henderson Crosthwaite & Co
Central House, Medwin Walk, Horsham RH12 1AG
Telephone: (0403) 61167
Henderson Crosthwaite & Co (Far East)
Elizabeth House, 3rd Floor, 250 Gloucester Road, Hong Kong
Henderson Crosthwaite & Co (Far East)
Kowa 35 Building, 14-14 Akasaka 1-Chome, Minato-ku, Tokyo 107, Japan
Partners: Twenty-nine

HESELTINE MOSS & CO (B)
30-31 Friar Street, Reading RG1 1AH
Telephone: (0734) 595511. Telex: 847739
Other Offices:
Lawrence House, 3-4 Trump Street, London EC2V 8DH
Telephone: 01-606 1401. Stx: 2477. Telegrams: Heseltine London EC2
2 Beaufort Buildings, Spa Road, Gloucester GL1 1XB
Telephone: (0452) 25444
112 Bartholomew Street, Newbury RG14 5DT
Telephone: (0635) 41385
4 King Edward Street, Oxford OX1 4HJ
Telephone: (0865) 243581
2 Imperial Square, Cheltenham GL50 1QB
Telephone: (0242) 45858
Stock Exchange Buildings, St Nicholas Street, Bristol BS1 1TW
Telephone: (0272) 276521
Devonshire House, Greyfriars Road, Cardiff CF1 3LB
Telephone: (0222) 34061. Telex: 497063
6 Caer Street, Swansea SA1 1DD
Telephone: (0792) 54907. Telex: 48394
60a North Street, Chichester, Sussex PO19 1NB
Telephone: (0243) 786472
Partners: Twenty-one

HICHENS, HARRISON & CO (B)
Bell Court House, 11 Blomfield Street, London EC2M 1LB
Telephone: 01-588 5171/1936
Stx: 7797/7798/5236. Stx (Dealers): 4235/4236
Telegrams: Hichens London EC2. Telex: 01 318 7711 CODE H126

Partners: Five

HILL OSBORNE & CO (B)
Royal Insurance Building, Silver Street, Lincoln LN2 1DU
Telephone: (0522) 28244
Other Offices:
Permanent House, Horsefair Street, Leicester LE1 5BU
Telephone: (0533) 23468 (administration)
(0533) 29185 (clients)
Warnford Court, Throgmorton Street, London EC2M 2AT
Telephone: 01-628 2205
17 York Place, Scarborough YO11 2NP
Telephone: (0723) 372478/9
Partners: Seven

HILLMAN CATFORD BOARD & CO (B)
45 St Nicholas Street, Bristol BS1 1TX
Telephone: (0272) 291352/24051
Partners: Three

HOARE GOVETT LD (B)
Limited Corporate Member
Heron House, 319-325 High Holborn, London WC1V 7PB
Telephone: 01-404 0344. Stx: 4296/4297/4298/4299
Stx (Dealers): 2426/2427/2428/4161/4164
Telegrams: Auresco London WC1. Telex: 885474
Stock Deliveries:
27 Throgmorton Street, London EC2N 2AN
Other Offices:
Hoare Govett (Far East) LD   30th Floor
Edinburgh Tower, The Landmark, Central, Hong Kong
Telephone: 5 256291/7
Telegrams: Auresco Hong Kong. Telex: HX 74111
Hoare Govett (Far East) LD
Singapore Representative Office, 10-09 Robina House
1 Shenton Way, Singapore 0106
Telephone: 224 7066. Telex: RS 20763
Hoare Govett (Far East) LD
Tokyo Representative Office, 556 Nippon Building
6-2 Ohtemachi, 2-chome, Chiyoda-ku, Tokyo 100
Telephone: 246-2901
Hoare Govett Incorporated
535 Madison Avenue, NY 10022, New York, USA
Telephone: (212) 355 2262. Telex: 237449
Directors: Six
Associated Members with Personal Liability: Twenty-six

HOARE GOVETT (JERSEY) LTD (B)
Limited Corporate Member
Stock Exchange Trading Subsidiary of Hoare Govett Limited
PO Box 387, Charles House, Charles Street, St Helier, Jersey, Channel Islands
Telephone: (0534) 77548. Telex: 4192171
Directors: Two

HOARE GOVETT (MONEYBROKING) LD (B)
Limited Corporate Member
Stock Exchange Trading Subsidiary of Hoare Govett Limited
27 Throgmorton Street, London EC2N 2AN

Telephone: 01-404 0344; 01-628 6601/6620
Stx: 3296/3297. Telex: 885474
Directors: Three

HORNE & MacKINNON (B)
60 Union Street, Aberdeen AB9 1DH
Telephone: (0224) 640222
Partners: Two

HOWITT & PEMBERTON (B)
PO Box 85, 17th Floor, Royal Exchange House, Boar Lane, Leeds LS1 5NS
Telephone: (0532) 439011. Telegrams: Howitt Leeds
Partners: Two

ILLINGWORTH & HENRIQUES (B)
PO Box 419, 38/40 Kennedy Street, Manchester M60 2BP
Telephone: 061-236 8521
Stx: 231. Stx (Dealers): 232
Other Offices:
Wardgate House, 59a London Wall, London EC2M 5UA
Telephone: 01-638 0801. Stx: 3546/3547/3548
Post Office Chambers, Court Row, Ramsey, Isle of Man
Telephone: 813782/812925
Partners: Nine

IRELAND (W.H.) & CO (B)
Dennis House, Marsden Street, Manchester M2 1HL
Telephone: 061-832 2174 (9 lines); 061-834 6325
Stx: 230. Telegrams: Whireland Manchester
Partners: Two

JACOBSON TOWNSLEY & CO (B)
Fourth Floor, Friars House, 39-41 New Broad Street, London EC2M 1NH
Telephone: 01-638 6671/01-588 1006 (general office)
Stx: 5195. Stx (Dealers): 4577/4578/4579/4291/4292/4293
Telex: 888948
Other Office:
28 Rue de Bourg, 1002 Lausanne, Switzerland
Telephone: 010 4121 20 79 13
Partners: Four

JAMES (ROY) & CO (B)
Stock Exchange Buildings, 33 Great Charles Street
Queensway, Birmingham B3 3JS
Telephone: 021-236 8131. Stx: 234/275
Partners: Four

JAY (G.H. & A.M.) (B)
61 Cheapside, London EC2
Telephone: 01-248 0081. Stx: 3061
Telegrams: Duty London EC2
Partners: Two

JENKINS (S.) & SON (J)
Warnford Court, London EC2
Telephone: 01-628 7588/0233. Stx: 2327
Partners: Four

JOLLIFFE FLINT & CROSS (B)
Jacey House, Lansdowne, Bournemouth BH1 2PP

Telephone: (0202) 25682
Other Office:
38 Parkstone Road, Poole BH15 2PG
Telephone: (0202) 676433
Partners: Two

KEITH BAYLEY ROGERS & CO (B)
194-200 Bishopsgate, London EC2M 4NR
Telephone: 01-623 2400. Stx: 3261
Telex: 888437
Other Office:
9 Devonshire Street, Carlisle CA3 8LG
Partners: Fourteen

KEMP, MITCHELL & CO (B)
62-64 Moorgate, London EC2R 6EL
Telephone: 01-628 8991. Stx: 3524
Telegrams: Gitnal London EC2. Telex: 884057
Partners: Four

KITCAT & AITKEN (B)
17th Floor, The Stock Exchange, London EC2N 1HB
Telephone: 01-588 6280. Stx: 2727
Telegrams: Kayanday London EC2. Telex: 888297/885419
Other Office:
Kitcat, Aitken & Safran LD
770 Lexington Avenue, New York, NY 10021, USA
Telephone: 0101 212 308 4949
Partners: Twenty-four
Limited Partner: One

LAING & CRUICKSHANK (B)
Unlimited Corporate Member
Piercy House, Copthall Avenue, London EC2R 7BE
Telephone: 01-588 2800. Stx: 4822
Telegrams: Laingstock Ldn. Telex: 888397/8
Other Offices:
10 Gildredge Road, Eastbourne, Sussex
Telephone: (0323) 20893/31656
41 Bridge Street, Taunton, Somerset
Telephone: (0823) 54351
14 Castle Lane, Belfast BT1 5DE
Telephone: (0232) 221002
De Quincey House, 48 West Regent Street, Glasgow G2 2RB
Telephone: 041-333 9323
35-39 Colomberie, St Helier, Jersey, Channel Islands
Telephone: (0534) 34321
Shareholders: Fifty-four

LAURENCE, PRUST & CO (B)
Basildon House, 7-11 Moorgate, London EC2R 6AH
Telephone: 01-606 8811. Stx: 4631
Telegrams: Laurence London EC2. Telex: 888570
Other Office:
2-4 Oldknow Road, Marple, Stockport, Cheshire
Telephone: 061-427 0456
Partners: Twenty-nine

LAURIE MILBANK & CO (B)
Portland House, 72-73 Basinghall Street, London EC2V 5DP
Telephone: 01-606 6622. Stx: 3388
Telegrams: Lauriemil London EC2. Telex: 887231
Partners: Thirty-three

LAURIE MILBANK & CO (JERSEY) (B)
Sister Partnership of **Laurie Milbank & Co**
Ordnance House, 31 Pier Road, St Helier, Jersey, Channel Islands
Telephone: (0534) 76774
Partners: Thirty-three

LAWS & CO (B)
30 Queen Charlotte Street, Bristol BS1 4DU
Telephone: (0272) 293901
Partners: Five

LE MARE MARTIN & CO (B)
City Gate House, 4th Floor, 39-45 Finsbury Square, London EC2A 1LE
Telephone: 01-628 9472 (8 lines). Stx: 3477
Telegrams: Lemare London EC4. Telex: 888710
Partners: Six

LE MASURIER JAMES & CHINN (B)
PO Box 16, 29 Broad Street, St Helier, Jersey, Channel Islands
Telephone: (0534) 72825 (8 lines)
Telegrams: Stocks Jersey. Telex: 4192134 Stks Jy
Partners: Five

LEWIS (E.R.) & CO (B)
Salisbury House, London Wall, London EC2M 5RE
Telephone: 01-628 0721. Stx: 3222
Telegrams: Edluis London Telex. Telex: 886931
Partners: Four

LLEWELLYN GREENHALGH & CO (B)
20 Mawdsley Street, Bolton BL1 1LF
Telephone: (0204) 21697/8
Partners: Two

LOVE (ALEX) ROGERS & CO (B)
37 Castle Street, Salisbury, Wiltshire SP1 1UB
Telephone: (0722) 335211
Partners: Two

LYDDON & CO (B)
113-116 Bute Street, Cardiff CF1 1QS
Telephone: (0222) 48000
Other Offices:
33 Mansel Street, Swansea SA1 1EB
Telephone: (0792) 54068
2-6 Austin Friars, London EC2N 2EE
Telephone: 01-628 5573. Stx: 7091
Telex: 883213
Partners: Eight

McCAW FLEMING & JUDD (B)
Unlimited Corporate Member
Aston House, Astons Place, Dublin 2
Telephone: Dublin 776941

Telegrams: Stocks Dublin. Telex: 25752
Shareholders: Four

McKEAN (R.N.) & CO (B)
11 Grove Place, Bedford
Telephone: (0234) 51131
Partners: Three

McLEAN (R.A.) & CO (J)
44 West George Street, Glasgow G2 1DW
Telephone: 041-332 5311/248/6587 (Dealers)
     041-332 5110 (Checking)
Stx: 271. Stx (Dealers) 325
Telegrams: Fraction. Telex: 77336
Partners: Four

McLELLAN BALLARD & CO (B)
Saxon House, 2 Railway Road, off Wellington Road South
Stockport, Cheshire SK1 3SW
Telephone: 061-480 3906/3035
Partners: Two

MAGENNIS & CO (B)
43 Lower Mill Street, Newry BT34 1AH
Telephone: (0693) 4314
Partners: Two

MAGUIRE McCANN MORRISON & CO (B)
Stock Exchange Building, 12 Anglesea Street, Dublin 2
Telephone: Dublin 771341
Telex: 25794
Other Offices:
46 Cecil Street, Limerick
Telephone: Limerick 44065
Telex: 26970
12 Marlboro Street, Cork
Telephone: Cork 20697
Telex: 26158
Partners: Eight

MARGETTS & ADDENBROOKE (B)
65 London Wall, London EC2M 5TU
Telephone: 01-588 0421
Stx: 7651/7652/7653. Stx (Dealers): 7655/7656
General Offices:
3rd Floor, 65 London Wall, London EC2M 5TU
Stx: 7654
Other Offices:
York House, 38 Great Charles Street, Queensway, Birmingham B3 3JU
Telephone: 021-236 1365/8386
Stx: 238/239/265/266
St Cuthberts House, Upper King Street, Norwich
Telephone: (0603) 619123
Partners: Eleven

MARSHALL & CO (B)
Jamaica Buildings, St Michaels Alley, London EC3V 9DS
Telephone: 01-621 1022 (Office)
     01-588 2056/1986/2102 (Dealers)

Stx: 4078. Stx (Dealers); 2381
Partners: Three

MATTHEWS (E.F.) & CO (B)
Colne House, 5 George Street, Colchester CO1 1TR
Telephone: (0206) 549831
Stx: 4189. Stx (Dealers): 4596
Partners: Four

MESSEL (L.) & CO (B)
3rd Floor, Winchester House, 100 Old Broad Street, London EC2P 2HX
Telephone: 01-606 4411. Stx: 4717
Telegrams: Messel London EC2
Telex: 884591 (Dealers); 883004 (Office)
General Office:
4th Floor, Winchester House, 100 Old Broad Street, London EC2P 2HX
Partners: Forty-two

MIDGLEY (E.) & CO (B)
Auburn House, 8 Upper Piccadilly, Bradford BD1 3PA
Telephone: (0274) 728866. Telegrams: Alert
Partners: Two

MILLS DUTTON & CO (B)
Lyndale House, 71 Queens Road, Oldham OL8 2BA
Telephone: 061-624 4651
Partners: Two

MILNES LUMBY BUSTARD (B)
Martins Building, 4 Water Street, Liverpool L2 3UF
Telephone: 051-236 9891. Stx: 260/274
Telegrams: Harbinger
Partners: Six

MILTON MORTIMER & CO (B)
21 Southernhay West, Exeter EX1 1PR
Telephone: (0392) 76244/5; 58255/6
Other Office:
Holland Walk, 74 High Street, Barnstaple, Devon EX31 1HX
Telephone: (0271) 71199
Partners: Four

MONTAGU LOEBL STANLEY & CO (B)
31 Sun Street, London EC2M 2QP
Telephone: 01-377 9242. Stx: 4247
Telegrams: Monlostan London EC2
Telex: 885941
Partners: Eighteen

MOORE GAMBLE CARNEGIE & CO (B)
24 Anglesea Street, Dublin 2
Telephone: Dublin 773914
Partners: Two

MORROGH (W. & R.) (B)
74 South Mall, Cork
Telephone: Cork 20647
Telex: 26145
Partners: Three

MOULSDALE (J)
Tithebarn House, Tithebarn Street, Liverpool L2 2PG
Telephone: 051-227 2705 (Office)
            051-227 5571 (Dealers)
Stx: 279. Stx (Dealers): 327 (5 lines)
Telex: 627360
Partners: Seven

MULLENS & CO (B)
15 Moorgate, London EC2R 6AN
Telephone: 01-638 4121. Stx: 7381
Telegrams: Mulmars London EC2
Telex: 888279
Partners: Sixteen

MURPHY (DENNIS) CAMPBELL & CO (B)
78 Queen Victoria Street, London EC4N 4SU
Telephone: 01-248 7255. Stx: 2101
Telegrams: Denmurph London EC4
Partners: Five

MURRAY & CO (B)
Beaufort House, 94-96 Newhall Street, Birmingham B3 1PE
Telephone: 021-236 0891. Stx: 260
Telex: 338397 REF MC
Other Offices:
Portland House, 22 Newport Road, Cardiff CF2 1DB
Telephone: (0222) 493618
City Gate House, 5th Floor, 39-45 Finsbury Square, London EC2A 1PX
Telephone: 01-588 2688. Stx: 4417
Partners: Seven

MURRAY (WILLIAM) (B)
1 Albyn Terrace, Aberdeen AB9 1RU
Telephone: (0224) 641307. Telex: 739148
Partners: Two

NEILSON HORNBY CRICHTON & CO (B)
State House, 22 Dale Street, Liverpool L69 2DD
Telephone: 051-236 6666
Stx: 270. Stx (Dealers): 269
Telegrams: Abgra Liverpool
Other Office:
Barclays Bank Chambers, Queens Square
Bowness-on-Windermere, Cumbria
Telephone: (09662) 2141/2
Partners: Five

NICHOLSON, BARBER & CO (B)
PO Box 132, Fargate Court, Fargate, Sheffield S1 1LE
Telephone: (0742) 755100. Stx: 238 (Manchester code)
Stx (Dealers): 237 (Manchester code)
Telegrams: Nikola Sheffield
Partners: Four

NIVISON (R) & CO (B)
25 Austin Friars, London EC2N 2JB
Telephone: 01-588 7244. Stx: 4401
Telegrams: Nivison London Telex

Telex: 885893
Partners: Ten

NORTHCOTE & CO (B)
119-125 Finsbury Pavement, London EC2A 1JJ
Telephone: 01-628 8121; 01-628 0202. Stx: 2111
Telegrams: Northality London EC2. Telex: 883540
Partners: Eight

O'BRIEN & TOOLE (B)
2 College Street, Dublin 2
Telephone: Dublin 778797/777556/770128/778303
Partners: Two

ORME & CO (B)
Warnford Court, Throgmorton Street, London EC2N 2BD
Telephone: 01-638 0991. Stx: 2117/2118
Telegrams: Ormeshare London EC2. Telex: 885216
Partners: Two

PARSONS & CO (B)
100 West Nile Street, Glasgow G1 2QU
Telephone: 041-332 8791. Stx: 264/265
Telegrams: Pageant Glasgow
Other Offices:
25 Albyn Place, Aberdeen AB1 1YL
Telephone: (0224) 29345
51 Meadowside, Dundee DD1 9PQ
Telephone: (0382) 21081
6 Walker Street, Edinburgh EH3 7LA
Telephone: 031-226 4466
84-86 Warnford Court, Throgmorton Street, London EC2
Telephone: 01-588 4302. Stx: 7341
Partners: Eleven

PEMBER & BOYLE (B)
PO Box 435, 30 Finsbury Circus, London EC2P 2HB
Telephone: 01-638 6242. Telex: 888626
Partners: Fourteen

PENNEY EASTON & CO (B)
PO Box 112, 24 George Square, Glasgow G2 1EB
Telephone: 041-248 2911. Stx: 266
Telegrams: Penney. Telex: 777967 (code 390)
Other Offices:
1-2 Finsbury Square, London EC2A 1AU
Telephone: 01-628 9321. Stx: 3551
Telegrams: Decastello London EC2
Telex: 24224 (ref: 420)
21 Dublin Street, Edinburgh EH1 3RF
Telephone: 031-556 1195
15 Barnton Street, Stirling FK8 1HF
Telephone: (0786) 3817
4 Charlotte Street, Perth PH1 5LL
Telephone: (0738) 37441
15 Wynnstay Road, Colwyn Bay, North Wales LL29 8NN
Telephone: (0492) 30354

1-2 Collingwood Buildings, Collingwood Street
Newcastle-upon-Tyne NE1 1JF
Telephone: (0632) 619957
Partners: Twenty-one

PHILLIPS & DREW (B)
120 Moorgate, London EC2M 6XP
Telephone: 01-628 4444. Stx: 4774
Telegrams: Phildrew London EC2
Telex: 291163
Other Offices:
Phillips & Drew
Regent House, 1 Hubert Road, Brentwood, Essex CM14 4QQ
Telephone: (0277) 222222. Telex: 99329/995986
Phillips & Drew
60 Halkett Place, St Helier, Jersey, Channel Islands
Telephone: (0534) 76061. Telex: 4192202
Phillips & Drew International LD
28th Floor, Tower 56, 126 East 56th Street, New York 10022, NY, USA
Partners: Sixty-two

PILLING TRIPPIER & CO (B)
12-14 St Anns Square, Manchester M2 7HT
Telephone: 061-832 6581. Stx: 279
Other Office:
21 The Butts, Rochdale OL16 1EZ
Telephone: (0706) 46951
Partners: Three

PINCHIN DENNY & CO (J)
Salisbury House, London Wall, London EC2
Telephone: 01-628 9633. Stx: 4747
Partners: Forty
Limited Partner: One

POPE (P.H.) & SON (B)
6 Pall Mall, Hanley, Stoke-on-Trent
Telephone: (0782) 25154
Telegrams: Pope Hanley
Partners: Two

PORTER & IRVINE (B)
18 & 19 College Green, Dublin 2
Telephone: Dublin 779881/3, 771741/2
Telex: 24480
Partners: Two

PUCKLE (GUY) & CO (B)
Warnford Court, London EC2N 2AT
Telephone: 01-628 6591. Stx: 2055
Telegrams: Dateless London
Telex: 885780
Partners: Five

PULLEY (CHARLES T.) & CO (J)
40 Bucklersbury, London EC4
Telephone: 01-236 2647/2648/2649/2640
Stx: 3281
Partners: Three

QUILTER GOODISON & CO (B)
Garrard House, 31-45 Gresham Street, London EC2V 7LH
Telephone: 01-600 4177. Stx: 4833
Telegrams: Quilbert London EC2. Telex: 883719/886134
Partners: Twenty-nine

RAMSDEN (ROBERT) & CO (B)
PO Box B16, 1st Floor, Estate Buildings
Railway Street, Huddersfield HD1 1NE
Telephone: (0484) 21501 (3 lines)
Telegrams: Arcade Huddersfield
Partners: Two

RAPHAEL, ZORN (B)
10 Throgmorton Avenue, London EC2N 2DP
Telephone: 01-628 4000
Stx: 7061/7062/7063/7064/7065/7066
Telegrams: Raphael London EC2. Telex: 885516
Partners: Fourteen

RATTLE (HAROLD) & CO (J)
Salisbury House, London Wall, London EC2M 5QQ
Telephone: 01-588 1605/1419 (Dealers)
01-588 0256/1164/1102
Telegrams: Rattle London
Stx: 4391. Telex: 8811498
Partners: Six

REDMAYNE-BENTLEY (B)
Merton House, Albion Street, Leeds LS1 6AG
Telephone: (0532) 436941
Partners: Three

RENSBURG & CO (B)
Silkhouse Court, Tithebarn Street, Liverpool L2 2NH
Telephone: 051-227 2030. Stx: 241/261/267/268
Telegrams: Renliv G
Other Offices:
14-16 Queensgate, Bradford BD1 1RB
Telephone: (0274) 729406. Telex: 51242
11 Park Square, Leeds LS1 2NG
Telephone: (0532) 445895
Partners: Fifteen

RIADA & CO (B)
28-29 Grafton Street, Dublin 2
Telephone: Dublin 716722
Partners: Three

RICHARDSON CHUBB & CO (B)
5 High West Street, Dorchester, Dorset DT1 1UJ
Telephone: (0305) 65252. Stx (Dealers): 7263
Partners: Three

ROBSON COTTERELL LD (B)
Limited Corporate Member
Bourne Chambers, St Peters Road, Bournemouth BH1 2JX
Telephone: (0202) 27581. Stx: 4502/4504/4522
Telegrams: Security Bournemouth UK. Telex: 41168/418297

Other Office:
12 Haven Road, Canford Cliffs, Poole, Dorset BH13 7LP
Directors: Two

ROWE & PITMAN (B)
City-Gate House, 39-45 Finsbury Square, London EC2A 1JA
Telephone: 01-606 1066. Stx: 3851
Telex: 8952485
Other Offices:
Rowe & Pitman Inc
24 California Street, San Francisco, California 94111-4853, USA
Telephone: (415) 433 2216. Telex: 470228
Rowe & Pitman Inc
31 Milk Street, Boston, Massachusetts 021 09, USA
Telephone: (617) 451 0490. Telex: 45430013
Rowe & Pitman (South Africa) Pty LD
45 Commissioner Street, Johannesburg 2001, South Africa
Telephone: (2711) 838 1927/9. Telex: 80251
Rowe & Pitman (Far East) LD
1414 Connaught Centre, Hong Kong
Telephone: (8525) 224123. Telex: 83495
Rowe & Pitman (Far East) LD
Imperial Tower 8F, 8C123, 1-1 Uchisaiwai-cho
1-Chome, Chiyoda-ku, Tokyo, Japan 100
Telephone: (813) 591 4201. Telex: 32695
Partners: Thirty-six
Limited Partner: One

ROWE & PITMAN INTERNATIONAL (B)
Unlimited Corporate Member
Stock Exchange Trading Subsidiary of Rowe & Pitman
City-Gate House, 39-45 Finsbury Square, London EC2A 1JA
Telephone: 01-606 1066. Stx: 3851
Telex: 8952485
Directors: Four

ROWE & PITMAN MONEYBROKING (B)
Unlimited Corporate Member
Stock Exchange Trading Subsidiary of Rowe & Pitman
16th Floor, The Stock Exchange, London EC2N 1HJ
Telephone: 01-628 2251. Stx: 3851
Telex: 8952485
Directors: Four

SABIN BACON WHITE & CO (B)
Stock Exchange Buildings, 33 Great Charles Street
Queensway, Birmingham B3 3JW
Telephone: 021-236 5591. Stx: 235
Partners: Six

SAVORY (E.B.) MILLN & CO (B)
3 London Wall Buildings, London EC2M 5PU
Telephone: 01-638 1212. Stx: 2744
Telegrams: Saymilln London Telex
Telex: 884287
General Office:
3rd Floor, 5 London Wall Buildings, London EC2M 5PU
Partners: Twenty-four

SCHAVERIEN & CO (B)
18½ Sekforde Street, London EC1R 0HN
Telephone: 01-251 1626. Stx: 3811
Telegrams: Shavab London EC1. Telex: 262120
Stock Deliveries:
4th Floor, 2-12 Wilson Street, London EC2
Partners: Nine
Limited Partner: One

SCHWEDER (PAUL E.) MILLER & CO (B)
46-50 Sun Street, London EC2M 2PX
Telephone: 01-588 5600. Stx: 2277
Telegrams: Schwedism Stock London
Telex: 886793
Partners: Twelve

SCOTT GOFF LAYTON & CO (B)
Salisbury House, London Wall, London EC2M 5SX
Telephone: 01-628 4433. Stx: 4141
Telegrams: GOFBROKA London EC2. Telex: 886594
Other Office:
6th Floor, Metboard House, 29 de Beer Street
Braamfontein 2001, South Africa
Partners: Twenty-four
Limited Partners: Three

SCRIMGEOUR KEMP-GEE & CO (B)
4th Floor, 20 Copthall Avenue, London EC2R 7JS
Telephone: 01-600 7595. Stx: 4331
Telegrams: Dogfox London EC2. Telex: 885171/887177
Other Office:
Tirrem House, 16 High Street, Yarm-on-Tees, Cleveland TS15 9BN
Telephone: (0642) 783436. Telex: 587210
Partners: Sixty-six

SCRIMGEOUR KEMP-GEE (JERSEY) & CO (B)
Sister Partnership of **Scrimgeour Kemp-Gee & Co**
PO Box 82, 1 Charing Cross, St Helier, Jersey, Channel Islands
Partners: Sixty-six

SELIGMANN RAYNER & CO (B)
Friendly House, 21-24 Chiswell Street, London EC1Y 4TU
Telephone: 01-606 2394. Stx: 2175
Telegrams: Selikoy Stock London
Other Offices:
Seligmann Harris & Co Inc
99 Wall Street, New York, NY 10005
Telephone: (212) 483 0878
Seligmann Harris & Co Inc
Friendly House, 21-24 Chiswell Street, London EC1Y 4TU
Telephone: 01-920 9641
Seligmann Rayner & Co
Stadhausquai 1, Postfach 8022, Zurich, Switzerland
Partners: Three
Limited Partner: One

SEYMOUR PIERCE & CO (B)
10 Old Jewry, London EC2R 8EA
Telephone: 01-628 4981. Stx: 3038

Telegrams: Spac Stock London
Partners: Eight

SHARP (ALBERT E.) & CO (B)
Edmund House, 12 Newhall Street, Birmingham B3 3ER
Telephone: 021-236 5801. Stx: 262
Telex: 336550
Other Office:
6-7 Queen Street, London EC4N 1SP
Telephone: 01-248 8676. Stx: 2277/2278
Partners: Fourteen

SHARP (JAMES) & CO (B)
2 Victoria Buildings, Silver Street, Bury, Lancashire BL9 0EP
Telephone: 061-764 4043/5. Stx: 280 (Manchester code)
Partners: Four

SHAW & CO (B)
4 London Wall Buildings, Blomfield Street, London EC2M 5NT
Telephone: 01-638 3644. Stx: 3197
Telegrams: Cybele London EC2. Telex: 888949/8956236
Partners: Eight

SHEPPARDS AND CHASE (B)
Clements House, Gresham Street, London EC2V 7AU
Telephone: 01-606 8099
Fax No. (Gp 3): 01-600 3386
Stx: 2755. Telegrams: Sheppelly London EC2
Telex: 886268/887091/887526
Other Offices:
Sheppards and Chase
41 Broad Street, St Helier, Jersey, Channel Islands
Telephone: (0534) 27276. Fax No. (Gp 3): (0534) 30185
Telegrams: Shepjy Jersey. Telex: 4192287
Sheppards and Chase
Suites 3/4E, PO Box 286, Hirzel Court
St Peter Port, Guernsey, Channel Islands
Telephone: (0481) 28950
Fax No. (Gp 2): (0481) 26008
Telex: 4191459
Sheppards and Chase (Overseas)
75 Montgomery Street, Jersey City, New Jersey 07302, USA
Telephone: (201) 333 2070. Telex: 239012/239018
Partners: Forty-one

SIDDALL (JOHN) & SON (B)
The Stock Exchange, Norfolk Street, Manchester M2 1DS
Telephone: 061-832 7471 (4 lines). Stx: 281
Telegrams: Sidd Manchester
Other Office:
6 Broad Street Place, London EC2
Partners: Two

SIMON & COATES (B)
1 London Wall Buildings, London EC2M 5PT
Telephone: 01-588 3644. Stx: 2700
Telegrams: Coates London EC2M 5PT
Telex: 885128
Other Office:

Simon & Coates (Overseas)
1508 Prince's Building, Hong Kong
Partners: Twenty-eight
Limited Partner: One

SMITH BROS plc (J)
Limited Corporate Member
241 Salisbury House, London Wall, London EC2M 5QT
Telephone: 01-628 2080. Stx: 3877
Telex: 884410
Directors: Thirteen
Associated Members with Personal Liability: Four

SMITH (JOHN S) & CO (B)
D Floor, Milburn House, Newcastle-upon-Tyne NE1 1LZ
Telephone: (0632) 326695
Partners: Three

SMITH KEEN CUTLER (B)
Exchange Buildings, Stephenson Place, Birmingham B2 4NN
Telephone: 021-643 9977. Telex: 336730
Other Office:
52 Cornhill, London EC3V 3NR
Telephone: 01-623 9483. Stx: 7294/7270
Partners: Eleven

SOLOMONS ABRAHAMSON & CO (B)
1-3 Westmoreland Street, Dublin 2
Telephone: Dublin 778264/776141
Telegrams: Solus Dublin
Partners: Two

SPEIRS & JEFFREY (B)
36 Renfield Street, Glasgow G2 1NA
Telephone: 041-248 4311
Stx: 268. Stx (Dealers); 267/277
Telegrams: Interest Glasgow. Telex: 777902
Partners: Four

SPRINGER BALE & LEWIS (B)
110 Warnford Court, Throgmorton Street, London EC2
Telephone: 01-628 9941/8322. Stx: 2274/2275
Telegrams: Spribale Stock London
Partners: Two

STANCLIFFE TODD & HODGSON (B)
PO Box 84, City House, 206/208 Marton Road
Middlesbrough, Cleveland TS4 2JE
Telephone: (0642) 249211. Telex: 587325
Other Offices:
23 Regent Street, Barnsley, South Yorkshire S70 2HH
Telephone: (0226) 82268/82277
1 Cecil Street, Carlisle, Cumbria CA1 1NL
Telephone: (0228) 21200/21422. Telex: 64340
Claremont House, Victoria Avenue, Harrogate, North Yorkshire HG1 1QQ
Telephone: (0423) 66071. Telex: 57661
Middleton Chambers, Lowgate, Hull, North Humberside HU1 1EA
Telephone: (0482) 226293/23935. Telex: 527063
57 John Street, Sunderland, Tyne-and-Wear SR1 1QR

Telephone: (0783) 657575. Telex: 538261
1-2 London Wall Buildings, London Wall, London EC2M 5PP
Telephone: 01-628 3480. Stx (Dealers): 4511/4516
Partners: Ten

STANLEY (CHARLES) & CO (B)
Garden House, 18 Finsbury Circus, London EC2M 7BL
Telephone: 01-638 5717. Stx: 3535
Telegrams: Chastons London EC2. Telex: 8952218
Other Offices:
PO Box 166, 1-3 Irish Place, Gibraltar
Telephone: Gibraltar 75181. Telex: 2361 BROKER GKD
9 Pembroke Street, Cambridge CB2 3QY
Telephone: (0223) 316726
13 Arcade Street, Ipswich, Suffolk IP1 1EX
Telephone: (0473) 210264
Partners: Twenty-two

STATHAM DUFF STOOP (B)
Capital House, 22 City Road, London EC1Y 2AJ
Telephone: 01-628 5070
Stx: 7373. Stx (Dealers): 3459
Telegrams: Stoop London EC1. Telex: 887220
Partners: Fourteen

STERNBERG THOMAS CLARKE & CO (B)
Provincial House, 218-226 Bishopsgate, London EC2M 4QD
Telephone: 01-247 8461. Stx: 2171/2172/2173
Stx (Dealers): 2174; Optns: 3470; Chkng: 4286/4287
Telegrams: Tomski London. Telex: 8812837
Partners: Seven
Limited Partners: Two

STEVENSON & BARRS (B)
PO Box 63, 10-12 St James Street, Derby DE1 1QY
Telephone: (0332) 47451/32425. Telegrams: Barrs Derby
Partners: Two

STIRLING HENDRY & CO (B)
Exchange House, 16 Royal Exchange Square, Glasgow G1 3AD
Telephone: 041-248 6033. Stx: 239/269/279
Telegrams: Stock Glasgow
Partners: Five

STOCK BEECH & CO (B)
Bristol & West Building, Broad Quay, Bristol BS1 4DD
Telephone: (0272) 20051. Stx: 3458
Telegrams: Spry Bristol. Telex: 44739
Other Offices:
Ground Floor, Warnford Court, Throgmorton Street, London EC2N 2AY
Telephone: 01-638 8471. Stx: 4275
Lloyds Bank Chambers, 75 Edmund Street, Birmingham B3 3HL
Telephone: 021-233 3211. Stx: 267
Partners: Eighteen

STOKES & KELLY BRUCE SYMES & WILSON (B)
Stock Exchange Buildings, 24 Anglesea Street, Dublin 2
Telephone: Dublin 770572/778457
Partners: Four

STOTT (R.L.) & CO (B)
Exchange House, 54-58 Athol Street, Douglas, Isle of Man
Telephone: (0624) 3701/2/3/4 (Office)
(0624) 26933/4/5 (Dealers)
Telex: 629623
Other Office:
77 Parliament Street, Ramsey, Isle of Man
Telephone: (0624) 813233
Partners: Five

STRAUSS TURNBULL & CO (B)
Unlimited Corporate Member
3 Moorgate Place, London EC2R 6HR
Telephone: 01-638 5699
Stx: 4733. Stx (Dealers): 4021
Telegrams: Strabul London EC2
Telex: 883201
Shareholders: Twenty-seven

SUTTON (FOWLER) & CO (B)
PO Box 10, 35 Bishop Lane, Hull HU1 1PA
Telephone: (0482) 25750
Other Office:
Pelham House, 1 Grosvenor Street, Grimsby, South Humberside
Telephone: (0472) 50232
Partners: Three

TEATHER & GREENWOOD (B)
Austin Friars House, 2-6 Austin Friars, London EC2N 2EE
Telephone: 01-628 0321. Stx: 4211/4213
Stx (Dealers): 5231; (Institutional): 4308
Telegrams: Thergre London EC2. Telex: 887246
Partners: Six

THOMPSON (R.J.) & CO (B)
76 Cannon Street, London EC4
Telephone: 01-248 2406. Stx: 4214
Telegrams: Arjaytee Stock London
Partners: Two

THORNTON (SPENCER) & CO (B)
Warnford Court, 29 Throgmorton Street, London EC2N 2JU
Telephone: 01-628 4411. Stx: 2121
Telegrams: Laborless London Telex. Telex: 883156/883850
Other Office:
Spenthorn House, 22 Cousin Lane, London EC4R 3TE
Telephone: 01-628 4411
Partners: Eleven

TILNEY & CO (B)
385 Sefton House, Exchange Buildings, Liverpool L2 3RT
Telephone: 051-236 6000. Stx: 275
Telegrams: Tilney Liverpool. Telex: 627367
Other Offices:
3rd Floor, Warnford Court, Throgmorton Street, London EC2N 2AT
Telephone: 01-638 0683 (Office)
01-638 3206 (Dealers)
Stx: 7461/7462. Stx (Dealers): 5046/5048/7087

Central Chambers, 15 Pride Hill, Shrewsbury SY1 1DQ
Telephone: (0743) 51374
Partners: Sixteen

TORRIE & CO (B)
6 Hope Street, Edinburgh
Telephone: 031-225 1766
Partners: Two

TREVOR MATTHEWS & CAREY LD (B)
Limited Corporate Member
PO Box 1, 21 Broad Street, Jersey, Channel Islands
Telephone: (0534) 73311. Telegrams: Trevor Jersey
Telex: 4192268
Other Office:
Trevor Matthews & Carey Ld
PO Box 8, Hirzel House, St Peter Port, Guernsey, Channel Islands
Telephone: (0481) 26511
Telegrams: Trevor Guernsey. Telex: 4191339
Directors: Eleven

VICKERS da COSTA (UK) LD (B)
Limited Corporate Member
Regis House, King William Street, London EC4R 9AR
Telephone: 01-623 2494. Fax No. (Gp 3): 01-626 3750
Stx: 7211. Telegrams: Vidacos London EC4
Telex: 888560/886004
Directors: Seven
Associated Member with Personal Liability: One

VIVIAN GRAY & CO (B)
Ling House, 10-13 Dominion Street, London EC2M 2UX
Telephone: 01-628 9311. Stx: 4377
Telegrams: Vitality London EC2. Telex: 887080
Other Offices:
Eagle Star House, Lemon Street, Truro, Cornwall
Telephone: (0872) 75454
35 Bridge Street, Hereford, Herefordshire
Telephone: (0432) 53491
Friars House, 39-41 New Broad Street, London EC2M 1NS
Telephone: 01-638 3056
Partners: Twenty

WAGNER (H. & R.) (B)
Moorgate Hall, 155-157 Moorgate, London EC2
Telephone: 01-606 9131. Stx: 4371
Telegrams: Posidonia Stock London
Telex: 885911/885912
Partners: Two

WALKER CRIPS WEDDLE BECK & CO (B)
Unlimited Corporate Member
Kemp House, 2nd Floor, 152-160 City Road, London EC1V 2PQ
Telephone: 01-253 7502. Stx: 4446
Telegrams: Reloan Stock London
Stock Deliveries:
c/o Messrs C. T. Pulley & Co

40 Bucklersbury, London EC4
Shareholders: Six
Limited Partner: One

WALTER WALKER & CO (B)
154 Bishopsgate, London EC2M 4XB
Telephone: 01-247 7631. Stx: 4541
Telegrams: Quietly Stock London (Office)
          Adduco Stock London (House)
Telex: 884451
Partners: Ten

WARD (WALTER) & CO (B)
Norfolk Chambers, 11 Norfolk Row, Sheffield S1 2PA
Stx: 233 (Manchester code). Stx (Dealers): 3191
Partners: Four

WATTERSON & COOK (B)
3rd Floor, 61 Cheapside, London EC2V 6AX
Telephone: 01-236 1607 (Office)
          01-638 8111 (Dealers)
Stx: 5290. Stx (Dealers): 7888
Partners: Two

WEDD DURLACHER MORDAUNT & CO (J)
Austral House, Basinghall Avenue, London EC2V 5EX
Telephone: 01-628 8080. Stx: 2626
Telegrams: Weddurl London EC2. Telex: 885967/885968
Partners: Sixty-seven
Limited Partner: One

WESTLAKE & CO (B)
Princess House, Eastlake Walk, Plymouth PL1 1HG
Telephone: (0752) 20971. Telex: 45438 PLYCOM
Partners: Eight

WHALE HARDAWAY & CO (B)
5 Park Hill Road, Torquay, Devon
Telephone: (0803) 22441/23098
Partners: Two

WHITE & CHEESEMAN LTD (J)
Limited Corporate Member
Warnford Court, Throgmorton Street, London EC2N 2AT
Telephone: 01-588 1647. Fax No: 01-588 0338
Stx: 3231. Telegrams: Wheese G London
Telex: 883971
Directors: Five

WIGRAM (ROBERT) & CO (B)
Princes House, 95 Gresham Street, London EC2V 7NA
Telephone: 01-600 5321/01-606 0321
Stx: 7596. Stx (Dealers): 3311. Telex: 291907
Partners: Eight

WILLIAMS DE BROE HILL CHAPLIN & COMPANY (B)
Unlimited Corporate Member
PO Box 515, Pinners Hall, Austin Friars, London EC2P 2HS
Telephone: 01-588 7511 (Office)
          01-588 1644/5 (Dealers)

Stx: 3841. Telegrams: Willdebroe London EC2
Telex: Willdebroe London 887084
Shareholders: Thirty-three

WILSHERE BALDWIN & CO (B)
19 The Crescent, King Street, Leicester LE1 6RX
Telephone: (0533) 541344
Partners: Three

WILSON & WATFORD (J)
Piercy House, 7 Copthall Avenue, London EC2
Telephone: 01-638 9201. Stx: 7311
Stx (Dealers): 3451 to 3456/4217/4218/4219
Partners: Seven

WISE SPEKE & CO (B)
Commercial Union House, 39 Pilgrim Street, Newcastle-upon-Tyne NE1 6RQ
Telephone: (0632) 611266. Telegrams: Wise Newcastle
Telex: 53429 PACE G
Other Offices:
City Gate House, 39-45 Finsbury Square, London EC2A 1PX
Telephone: 01-638 0189
Stx: 7457. Stx (Dealers): 7364/7365
Airedale House, Albion Street, Leeds, Yorkshire LS1 5AL
Telephone: (0532) 459341
103 Albert Road, Middlesbrough, Cleveland TS1 2PA
Telephone: (0642) 248431
Partners: Seventeen

WISHART BRODIE & CO (B)
43 Charlotte Square, Edinburgh EH2 4HL
Telephone: 031-225 2813/5; 031-225 2992
Stx: 225
Partners: Four
Limited Partner: One

WOOD (RUSSELL) & CO (B)
Kennet House, Kennet Wharf Lane, Upper Thames Street, London EC4V 3AJ
Telephone: 01-236 3761/6. Stx: 4404/4227/4234
Telegrams: Woodrus London EC4
Partners: Three

WOOD, MacKENZIE & CO (B)
Erskine House, 68-73 Queen Street, Edinburgh EH2 4NS
Telephone: 031-225 8525. Telegrams: Woodmack Edinburgh
Other Offices:
Wood, MacKenzie & Co
62-63 Threadneedle Street, London EC2R 8HP
Telephone: 01-600 3600. Stx: 7361
Telegrams: Woodmack London EC2. Telex: 883369
Wood, MacKenzie & Co Inc
280 Park Avenue, West Building, 27th Floor, New York, NY 10017, USA
Telephone: (212) 883 1900. Telex: 669117 WMINC UW
Partners: Forty-two

WOODCOCK DERRY & CO (J)
39 St Nicholas Street, Bristol BS1 1TU
Telephone: (0272) 20411. Stx: 7390
Other Office:

Stock Exchange Buildings, Great Charles Street, Birmingham B3 3JT
Telephone: 021-236 3643. Stx: 331
Partners: Five

WRIGHT (D.M.) & PARTNERS (B)
15 The Diamond, Londonderry
Telephone: (0504) 263344/264310
Partners: Two

Source: Stock Exchange

Section IV
List of Share Perks

Company	Brief Details of Benefits	Minimum Share-holding to Qualify
Ackrill Carr	Holders entitled to commission rebate of 50% of the Life Offices Association initial commission scale when they purchase interalia investment bonds, unit trusts and savings and pension plans.	1,000 Ordinary shares.
Alexanders Holdings	Discount of around 2% on all vehicles at dealerships listed below:— Alexanders of Edinburgh Ltd. Alexanders of Kirkintilloch Ltd. Alexanders of Greenock Ltd. Alexanders of Northampton Ltd.	2,000 Ordinary shares.
All England Tennis (Stock tightly held and not generally marketable) Cost of two Debentures for 1986/90 series in excess of £8,000.	One free Centre Court ticket per day for every one £50 Debenture held. (Minimum purchase is two Debentures.) Entry to Lounge and Buffet Bar at Centre Court, and reserved car parking space adjacent to the Centre Court (for a small fee). Priority for 1991/95 series.	Two £50 (nominal) non-interest bearing Wimbledon Debentures
Allied-Lyons	Celebration package for £7 when you take a Hushaway Weekend Break. One £3 discount voucher, two £1.50 vouchers for use in Allied-Lyons Restaurants. Periodical wine offers and discount vouchers on Victoria Wine purchases. (Reviewed in June)	No minimum.

159

Company	Brief Details of Benefits	Minimum Share-holding to Qualify
Appleton Holdings	'Bonusbreaks' book of vouchers issued entitling holder to free accommodation for two people at any of 124 hotels in Britain and Ireland for a maximum of 14 nights.	2,500 Ordinary shares.
A. Arenson (Holdings)	15% on 'Arvin' domestic furniture and 'Room-sets' bedroom furniture.	Ordinary and Preference shares – no minimum. Unit trusts and investment trusts with holdings may nominate beneficiary.
Asprey	Asprey card, sent when holding registered, giving 15% discount on most cash purchases from Aspreys in Bond Street and 153 Fenchurch Street.	375 Ordinary shares.
Associated British Foods	Gift of some of the company's product (approximately eight grocery items), at AGM. Worth approximately £5 to £6.	No minimum.
BSG International	Shareholders may contact company to obtain various discounts on their products, e.g. child safety seats and seat belts.	No minimum.
Barclays Unicorn Group	Special rates on a number of Cunard cruise holidays are available to investors.	All unit holders.
Barker & Dobson	20% discount on retail price of certain lines provided by Charbonnel et Walker Ltd.	No minimum. Ordinary 6¾% Ln. 12% Ln.
Barr and Wallace Arnold	7½% discount on package holidays on accommodation at Oswalds Hotel, Torquay. 10% dis-	250 Ordinary or 'A' shares.

	count on a new car, without trade-in, at any of the group's garages.	
Barratt Developments	Discount on purchase of new house. £500 per £25,000 or part thereof of the purchase of a Barratt property. Thus a shareholder purchasing a property for £30,000 would be entitled to a discount of £1,000.	1,000 Ordinary shares held at least 12 months.
Bass	Shareholder benefit card entitles holder to 15% discount off full tariff price at all Crest Hotels Monday to Thursday. On Friday, Saturday, Sunday and public holidays most Crest Hotels offer 'Two for the price of one' charging only the normal single price for a double or twin room. Holders are entitled to 15% off this rate, which is based on a 1-3 night stay exclusive of meals. Holders also enjoy 15% off all Crest Welcome Breaks. Prices for bed and breakfast only are available in London, Amsterdam and other Crest Hotels on the continent. 10% reduction in the cost of a Pontins UK holiday subject to availability for the shareholder and his family and/or friends.	50 Ordinary shares – shares or preference
Bassett Foods	Shareholders are invited to an Open Day (at either of the factories, to include lunch plus a gift of confectionery) plus an opportunity to purchase confectionery at discounted prices.	No minimum.
Beecham Group	Occasional wine offer.	No minimum.
Bellway	£500 – £2,500 discount on price of a new Bellway house. 10% discount on Nixon kitchen units.	1,000 Ordinary shares held for one year.

Company	Brief Details of Benefits	Minimum Share-holding to Qualify
Bentalls	Discount vouchers entitling shareholders to total discounts of £15 on purchases up to £150. Issued in May and valid until 31st January of the following year.	100 Ordinary shares.
B.L.	£100 discount on new car (additional to any terms negotiated initially with the dealer). This discount excludes VAT. Only one Shardis Authorisation form during period between each annual meeting.	1,000 Ordinary held at date of most recent General Meeting and held for six months.
Britannia Arrow Holdings	2% discount at all times on an investment in any of the group's unit trusts.	1,000 Ordinary shares on register for 12 months.
N. Brown Investments	20% discount on various items purchased from J. D. Williams and other mail order catalogues of the group. 20% discount on fashion wear of the group's Heather Valley (Woollens) subsidiary. Maximum discount allowable is £200.	No minimum.
Burton Group	Three vouchers usually issued in December, giving 20% discount at Burton, Top Shop, Evans, D. Perkins, Top Man, Principles and Peter Robinson.	No minimum.
C.G.A.	Free membership to CGA Members entitled to reduced rates on a wide range of goods and services.	100 Ordinary shares.
Cadbury Schweppes	Holders given samples of company's products at AGM.	No minimum.
Ciro	20% discount at some large stores where they operate jewellery counters.	500 Ordinary shares.

Company	Benefit	Qualification
Courts Furnishers	10% discount on furniture.	100 Ordinary/'A' ordinary on register for 3 months.
Cramphorn	10% discount on cash purchases excluding sale items at shops and garden centres. Discount card issued.	600 Ordinary shares held for one year.
Crossair (Swiss)	Flight vouchers with a value of SFr. 7.50, 75 and 150 issued depending on the number of shares held. Vouchers may be used as payment of air-fares up to a maximum of 50% of the Crossair fare (charter flights excluded) or as payment for excess baggage.	No minimum.
Debenhams	Shareholder card issued, giving credit limit of £3,000 and 7½% off marked prices at group's stores.	500 Ordinary shares on register for three months.
DFDS Danish Seaways (Shares tightly held and not generally marketable)	25% rebate on journeys made by shareholders plus one other person on Mondays, Tuesdays, Wednesdays and Thursdays, if booking made not MORE than eight days before date of departure. Reduction does not apply to cars and registered luggage. Documentary proof of share ownership must be shown before booking is made.	No minimum. Registered before 1st June any year.
Dominion International Group	Shareholder Benefit Scheme, with right to partici-pate in Annual Draw, held in the fourth quarter of each year. Six shareholders then picked to visit a location of their choice in the UK or overseas wherever Dominion has business interests. Share-holders are also entitled to £250 towards the expense of their funeral or cremation (on register by 30.6.82). This concession will expire on 30.6.87.	500 Ordinary shares held for at least 12 months prior to date of Draw.

Company	Brief Details of Benefits	Minimum Share-holding to Qualify
Edenspring Investments	Offer to shareholders to purchase ORIC personal computer and peripheral products at concessionary prices. (Shares dealt under Rule 535.2.)	No minimum.
Eldridge Pope	Discount on wines, beers, ciders and spirits. Details sent before Christmas.	No minimum.
Emess Lighting	25% discount on a range of light fittings.	100 Ordinary shares.

European Ferries	Subject to space availability, discount on the normal fare for the carriage of one private motor car (or motorised caravan or motorcycle) and four passengers (two fare-paying children count as one passenger), including the shareholder, on an unlimited number of return journeys on qualifying routes and sailings, as follows:—
	
	Dover to Calais, Boulogne, Zeebrugge
	  — 50% all sailings
	Felixstowe to Zeebrugge
	  — 50% excluding 'A' sailings
	Portsmouth to Cherbourg, Portsmouth to Le Havre
	  — 40% excluding 'A' sailings
	Cairnryan to Larne
	  — 25% all sailings
	No single journey or open-date tickets.
	Applications, specifying sailings and dates must be made by post at least 30 days before first date in July and August, otherwise seven days, to the company's shareholders' Concessions Department.
		300 Preference shares registered by 31st December any year.

P & O holders are entitled to the discount on the Boulogne and Le Havre routes for 1985 only.

Holders of 300 or more Preference shares will qualify for the full concessions up to 1.1.88. After then you will have to hold at least 600 Preference to qualify for the maximum discounts. If you have between 300 and 599 Preference shares you will qualify for half the value of the discount after 1.1.88.

Please note that preference is given to full fare paying passengers.

20% discount off the price of one room for maximum stay of three nights for one visit per person at the Magheramorne House Hotel, Co. Antrim.

Reduction on room rates at the Dover Motel from 1st October 1984 – 25th June 1985 (excluding Bank Holiday weekends).

Selection from an approved range of furniture and furnishings obtainable from a local Spanish supplier, to furnish new accommodation purchased at La Manga, completely free of charge. Refund of up to £500 if you buy an apartment at La Manga after a one or two week self-catering holiday at La Manga.

Sponsorship at University College, Buckingham.

---

200 Deferred shares
500 Preferred shares
on register by 4.1.85.

300 Preference shares.

300 Preference shares held for at least one year prior to 22nd May 1985.

1,000 Ordinary/Preference or combination of both, registered by 1.1.83 for entry in 1986.

165

Company	Brief Details of Benefits	Minimum Share-holding to Qualify
Ferguson Industrial Holdings	Free entry for up to four people to 12th Century Appleby Castle (Co's registered office) on presentation of a copy of the annual report. The grounds are open to the public throughout the summer months.	No minimum.
Fobel International	Special offers on a variety of goods, covering TV games, tele-text decoders, radio watches and view data printers, portable telephones and home computers.	No minimum.
Cecil Gee	Various discounts at Cecil Gee, Gee 2, Savoy Taylors Guild and Beale & Inman shops. One 10% discount voucher. Two 10% discount voucher. A further discount voucher is sent out for each additional 1,000 shares held. (Vouchers may be used during sales.) Discount vouchers are distributed once a shareholder has been on the register for six months.	500 shares. 1,000 shares.
The Gieves Group	20% discount on goods purchased from branches of Gieves & Hawkes. Shareholder's Concession Card issued.	600 Ordinary shares held for three months.
Grand Metropolitan Hotels	Voucher offering £4 off a meal for two at any Berni Inn. Various discounts on wine, mixed cases of wine and spirits, beer, lager, sherry, spirits and sports goods. 10% discount on Stardust and Camelot mini-holidays.	No minimum.

	10% discount on a Warner UK holiday. 10% discount on Travelscene holidays. Grand Metropolitan Account Card issued on request.	No minimum.
Greenall Whitley	10% discount on current G. W. or De Vere Hotel tariff. 10% discount on G.W. or De Vere Hotels 'Breakaway Weekend' rates. 10% discount on 'Before You Fly Package'. Periodic. 10% discount on one Summer and one Winter holiday publicised in the current Arrowsmith or Skyfares brochures — Flights from Manchester only.	400 Ordinary shares or 2,000 'A' Ordinary shares.
GRA Group	Invitation to shareholder and one guest to spend an evening at one of the stadiums. One free voucher for car park also sent.	No minimum.
Hawtin	20% discount on selected GUL Wetsuits.	No minimum.
Hawley Group	15% discount on any one purchase of Sharps fitted bedrooms, Dolphin Showers and Alpine Double Glazing installed at the address of the registered shareholder.	500 shares.
Henlys	Shareholders are offered any make of motor car from the manufacturers the company represents at attractive terms. Also holidays on the Norfolk Broads.	No minimum.
J. Hepworth	25% discount on one purchase in any Hepworth or Next shop.	500 Ordinary shares.

Company	Brief Details of Benefits	Minimum Share-holding to Qualify
Hillards	Discount at Hillards stores during the Christmas period. Five vouchers of £3 each off purchases exceeding £30. (Not on cigarettes of petrol.) Sent out with annual report and account. Share-holders attending AGM receive lunch.	200 Ordinary shares.
Higsons Brewery	£2 voucher redeemed when spending over £10 in Mellors off-licence. Special offers on wine.	No minimum.
Horizon Travel	10% discount on Horizon brochure prices, up to a total holiday value of £1,000. Available to one booking per shareholder in any year. Shareholder must travel. Only one concession per booking.	750 Ordinary, held for six months at date of departure.
Isle of Man Steam Packet (Shares tightly held and not generally marketable)	On application to head office, return ferry ticket(s) at the time of booking from Douglas to Liverpool, Ardrossan, Dublin, Llandudno, Fleetwood and Belfast. During June, July and August valid Mondays to Fridays only.	£250– £499 Ord Stk (1) £500– £999 Ord Stk (2) Over £1,000 Ord Stk (3)
Kean & Scott Holdings	15% discount on Sharps Fitted Bedrooms, Dolphin Showers and Alpine Double Glazing.	500 Ordinary shares
Kennedy Brookes	20% discount at any of their restaurants including Maxims in London. Credit card issued.	500 Ordinary shares.
John Kent	10% discount on purchases from 'John Kent' and 'Smith' branches. Discount card issued upon registration and renewed with annual report.	500 Ordinary shares.
Robert Kitchen Taylor (RKT)	£7 discount on an order of £15– £25 worth of group's underwear, including Damart, and outer-wear. £15 discount on an order over £25.	500 Ordinary shares.

Kursaal Company	Free admission to Dragonara Palace Casino, with a guest. 10% discount on Mediterranean Room or Marquis Room bills (except Saturdays), Lido admission and Reef Club subscriptions. 15% discount on summer rates, $33\frac{1}{3}$% discount on winter rates, on hotel stay at the Dragonara Palace Hotel on booking made direct with MAXOTELS offices in UK or Malta.	200 shares of any class.
Kwik-Fit (Tyres & Exhausts) Holdings	10% discount on any purchase worth £5 or more, from any of company's depots. Vouchers enclosed with report. Only one purchase per year.	100 Ordinary shares.
LWT (Holdings)	10% discount on holidays with Page & Moy Ltd., Harborough Marina Ltd., Cresta World Travel Ltd., and Sunspot Tours Ltd. Discount covers shareholder and family or friends travelling together on the same holiday.	No minimum.
Ladbroke Group	10% discount on hotels, motor inns & restaurants, and holiday villages. 7½% discount on marked prices at Lasky stores on all hi-fi, video and microcomputer products. Shareholders privilege card issued. 10% discount on annual membership *only* at the following snooker clubs. Blyth Snooker – Northumberland. Cueball Snooker Club – Glasgow, Kirkcaldy and Greenock. Cueball Snooker & Leisure Club – Paisley.	No minimum.
Leyland Paint & Wallpaper	10% discount at Leyland DIY shops.	No minimum.

Company	Brief Details of Benefits	Minimum Share-holding to Qualify
London & Midland Inds	Discount of 10% on Compton Buildings, Banbury windows, Banbury Homes & Gardens and Falcon Pipe Group.	No minimum.
London European Airways	Free parking at Luton Airport for first 48 hours when travelling on London European. One free return ticket for a shareholders companion travelling at least one way with the member on a London European Airways flight for every ten flights taken by member. Use of VIP lounges at Luton and Amsterdam. 20% discount on duty-free purchases.	5,000 Ordinary shares.
London & Northern Group	12½% discount on list prices of Weatherseal double glazing, patio doors, and replacement windows. Leaflet and form circulated to shareholders, or direct approach to Weatherseal.	250 Ordinary shares or 250 Preference. Employees of shareholding companies and institutions also eligible.
Lonrho	Periodical discount on Audi & Volkswagen motor cars. 20% discount on room rates in UK Metropole Hotels. 10% discount on 'Whileaway Holidays' at all UK hotels. 30% discount on full rater bedrooms at the Melville Hotel in Mauritius (valid for bookings through Kuoni Travel), excluding November and December. 15% discount at Brentfords. £20 off major service at a Dutton Forshaw garage.	At company's discretion. 100 shares on register by 1st March.
Manders Holdings	Discount of 25% on brushes, 20% on paint and 10% on both wallpaper and sundries. 'Trade cash card' sent to shareholders.	No minimum.

Manor National	Various discounts on new and used Ford and Austin Rover cars plus Land Rover and Range Rover vans. Discount on all types of insurance cover.	No minimum.
Maynards	10% discount on confectionery from Maynards during Christmas period. 25% discount on toys purchased from Zodiac Shops.	25 Ordinary shares.
Mellerware International	12% discount on Co's products (up to £250).	250 Ordinary shares.
Merrydown Wine	Approximately 20% discount on cases of wine and cider, inclusive of VAT. Shareholders invited to lunch and wine tasting after AGM.	No minimum.
Milletts Leisure	12½% discount on shop goods. Discount card provided.	No minimum.
Moss Bros	10% discount on all goods and services, not at sale or special promotion prices. Discount card sent to holder. Second card sent to shareholders spouse on request.	250 Ordinary shares held for six months.
Mount Charlotte Investments	10% discount on a 'Value Break'. 10% discount at all the Company's Hotels for Room & Breakfast. 15% discount on weekly terms for Full Board at the Company's five Family Holiday hotels. For terms other than Full Board the discount will be 10%. The discount does not apply to Self-Catering holidays. Holders may purchase Bronte Yorkshire Liqueur at special price. Shareholders privilege card enclosed with proxy form.	1,000 Ordinary shares on register by 1st March.
Norfolk Capital Group	Vouchers issued with annual report and accounts entitling shareholders to a 10% discount at the	No minimum.

171

Company	Brief Details of Benefits	Minimum Share-holding to Qualify
	group's Hotels and Restaurants. 5% discount on any Greatstay weekend booking and Norbreck Castle holiday package. Valid until 1.4.86.	
Park Food Group	20% discount on range of hampers.	No minimum.
Peninsular & Oriental Steam Navigation Company	Aberdeen–Lerwick (Shetlands) – 30% discount on all sailings except July & August. Scrabster–Stromness (Orkney) – 30% discount. Restricted to two round trips in a 12 month period, return journeys only. Shareholder must travel. Shareholders qualify as soon as their name is on the register. **Please note that preference on bookings will be to full fare paying passengers.**	200 Deferred shares. 500 Preferred shares.
Pentos	Holders may apply for a discount card allowing 10% off any cash purchase at companies book shops and at Athena Galleries.	500 Ordinary or Deferred shares or a combination.
Peters Stores	15% discount on all cash purchases at any branch (general clothing, industrial and protective clothing, camping, sailing and sports equipment). Card with report in November. Buffet lunch for shareholders attending AGM.	No minimum.
Pleasurama	£10 voucher sent with annual report for use as part payment towards meal for two or overnight stay at selected hotels.	No minimum.

Alfred Preedy & Sons

10% discount on purchases in excess of £3, at any of the group's 200 stores and shops, on all goods except cigarettes and tobacco, newspapers and magazines. (Goods include toys and games, books, records, artists' materials, china and glassware, sports equipment, confectionery, greeting cards.) Form with report.

250 Ordinary shares.

Prince of Wales Hotels

Vouchers despatched with annual report offering the following discounts:—
    15% on B & B rates.
    15% on Budget Breakaway Holidays.
    15% on Restaurant Bills.
Plus introductory vouchers for friends using the following discounts:—
    10% on Restaurant Bills.
    10% on Budget Breakaway Holidays.
Vouchers valid until 30.9.85.

No minimum.

Queens Moat Houses

Two courtesy cheques for £2 towards food and drink when taking a meal in a Queens Moat House hotel. One courtesy cheque worth £15 when taking Town & Country Classics weekend accommodation at a Queens Moat House hotel.

No minimum.

Rank Organisation

Holiday Scheme
10% discount on brochure price of OSL, Wings, Ellerman, Sunflight or Freshfields Holidays up to a maximum holiday value of £1,000 for a shareholder and his party. Only one concession per booking.
Shareholder must travel.

750 Ordinary shares on register for at least six months at the date of departure or the holder of any number of Ordinary shares for a continuous period of five years up to date of departure.

Company	Brief Details of Benefits	Minimum Share-holding to Qualify
	Hotels Scheme 10% discount on normal published tariff at any Rank Hotel. 10% discount on special weekend rates available at certain times of the year.	
Ranks Hovis McDougall	Hamper at AGM.	No minimum.
Austin Reed	15% discount but not on sale or special promotion prices.	500 Ordinary or 'A' ordinary shares.
Riley Leisure	Approximately 20% discount on billiard tables. Up to 25% discount on billiard cues. Free membership to any Riley Snooker Club.	No minimum.
Romney, Hythe & Dymchurch Light Railway Company (Shares tightly held and not generally marketable)	a) Free personal travel pass. b) as a) plus additional free pass for members of shareholder's family. c) as b) plus further pass for shareholders' guests and the right to hire a complete train once per year at no cost.	a) 100–499 Ord. shares. b) 500–4,999 Ord. shares. c) 5,000 shares or more.
Routledge & Kegan Paul (Shares tightly held)	25% discount on all books in stock. Orders placed with Trade Department at Henley-on-Thames.	250 Ordinary shares.
Savoy Hotel	Special offer 'Two's Company' at either The Savoy or Claridges, shareholders will receive a special allowance of £5 per person, per night. *(Concession reviewed in April)*	No minimum.
Securicor Group	Periodical discounts on communications equipment and at company's hotels in Coventry, Richmond and Rosshire. Details with annual report.	No minimum.

Company	Benefit	Minimum Holding
Sharpe & Fisher	10% discount on a purchase at one of group's DIY supermarkets and garden centres. Valid following account statement to 31st December.	No minimum.
Scottish & Newcastle Breweries	£21 voucher for use at Thistle Hotels enclosed with report. Selection of wines offered at a discount.	No minimum.
Sketchley	25% discount on normal cost of dry cleaning and ancillary services. Discount card issued on registration and thereafter automatic annual renewal (on 1st August) as long as qualifying shareholding remains on register.	300 Ordinary or Preference shares.
Southampton, Isle of Wight and South of England Royal Mail Steam Packet Co. (Shares tightly held and not generally marketable)	Free ferry tickets (Southampton to Cowes) and 50% discount on the Standard Single fare on hydrofoil services. Shareholder's pass issued when holding registered. There is no discount on motor cars.	2,400 Ordinary shares.
Spear & Jackson International	Discount on hand and garden tools, and a range of of lawnmowers. Application form enclosed with report.	No minimum.
Stakis	Vouchers despatched with Annual Report. 15% discount voucher on Stakis Summer holiday. £5 restaurant voucher. Voucher for £2 off six bottles of wine to the value of £15. Voucher offering six selected wines at £15.	100 Ordinary shares.
Stylo	Vouchers giving 20% discount on two separate purchases of shoes, sent with report. Company sends copy of latest report to new holders, therefore double vouchers in first year.	No minimum.

Company	Brief Details of Benefits	Minimum Share-holding to Qualify
Toye & Company	15% discount on purchases, from branches of Toye, Kenning & Spencer. (Civil and Military regalia, trophies, awards, medals, badges, jewellery, gold and silverware, cutlery, glassware, watches and clocks.) Does not apply to special offers or on postal orders. 'Special purchase card' issued once name is entered on register.	250 Ordinary shares. Institutional holders not eligible.
Trafalgar House	10% discount on most QE2 and Sagafjord World Cruises. 15% discount on most other cruises. 15% discount at Cunard hotels in UK and Caribbean.	250 Ordinary shares. Institutional and corporate holders may nominate one person to benefit.
Trusthouse Forte	10% discount on Leisure Gift cheques for maximum £2,000 value. Application form enclosed with report. Can be used in settlement of accounts at THF hotels, restaurants, and other THF establishments.	No minimum.
UBM Group	10% discount card for use at UBM Building Supplies branches.	No minimum.
E. Upton	15% discount on goods and services at company's stores excluding large electrical goods, e.g. Freezers, TV's and Audio equipment where the discount is 10%. 10% discount on carpets where free fitting is offered.	250 Ordinary or 'A' shares.
Valor	Various products offered to shareholders at special prices throughout the year.	No minimum.

Vaux Breweries	'Swallowcard' for use in Swallow hotels and restaurants, Anchor hotels and taverns. 10% discount on accommodation and meals. Vouchers for use in Swallow hotels providing discounted wines, Breakaway holidays, £25 off Leisure Club membership, etc. Twice yearly wine offer. Buffet lunch at AGM.	No minimum.
Vectis Stone Group	20% discount on tariff at Albion Hotel, Freshwater Bay during early and late season. Not available during Bank holidays. Details on request from the Albion Hotel.	No minimum.
Whitbread	Special booklet sent with annual report in June offering discounts on articles ranging from whisky to silver cufflinks.	No minimum.

Section V
Members of the
Unit Trust Association

Company Name	Address	Telephone No:
Abbey Unit Trust Managers Ltd	1-3 St Paul's Churchyard London EC4P 4DX	(01) 236 1555
Aitken Hume Funds (Management) Ltd	1 Worship Street London EC2A 2AB	(01) 638 6011
Allied Unit Trusts Ltd	Hambro Life Centre, Swindon Wiltshire SN1 1EL	(0793) 28291
Archway Unit Trust Managers Ltd	Southampton House, 317 High Holborn London WC1V 7NL	(01) 831 6233
Arkwright Management Ltd	Arkwright House, Parsonage Gardens Manchester M3 2LF	(061) 834 2332
Atlanta Unit Trust Managers Ltd	1 Founders Court London EC2R 7DB	(01) 600 8664/8
Barclays Unicorn Ltd	Unicorn House, 252-258 Romford Road London E7 9JB	(01) 534 5544
Baring Fund Managers Ltd	8 Bishopsgate London EC2N 4AE	(01) 283 8833
Barrington Management Company Ltd	PO Box 91, 59 Gresham Street London EC2P 2DS	(01) 606 4433

Bishopsgate Progressive Unit Trust Management Company Ltd	65 Holborn Street, London EC1A 2DR	(01) 248 4000
Britannia Group of Unit Trusts Ltd	74-78 Finsbury Pavement, London EC2A 1JD	(01) 588 2777
Brown Shipley Fund Management Ltd	Eldon House, 2-3 Eldon Street, London EC2M 7DU	(01) 377 1099
Buckmaster Management Company Ltd	The Stock Exchange, London EC2P 2JT	(01) 588 2868
Canada Life Unit Trust Managers Ltd	Granite House, 97-101 Cannon Street, London EC4N 5AD	(01) 238 9871
Clerical Medical Unit Trust Managers Ltd	Narrow Plain, Bristol BS2 0JH	(0272) 277719
Confederation Funds Management Ltd	Confederation Life House, 50 Chancery Lane, London WC2A 1HE	(01) 242 0282
County Bank Unit Trust Services Ltd	161 Cheapside, London EC2V 6EU	(01) 606 6060
Crown Unit Trust Services Ltd	Crown Life House, Crown Square, Woking, Surrey GU21 1XW	(04862) 24933
Dartington Unit Trust Management Ltd	Shinners Bridge, Dartington, Totnes, Devon TQ9 6JE	(0803) 862271
Discretionary Unit Fund Managers Ltd	Bilbao House, 36-38 New Broad Street, London EC2M 1NU	(01) 638 4485
Duncan Lawrie Fund Managers Ltd	1 Hobart Place, London SW1W 0HU	(01) 245 9321
EFM Unit Trust Managers Ltd	4 Melville Crescent, Edinburgh EH3 7JB	(031) 226 4931

179

Company Name	Address	Telephone No:
Equitable Units Administration Ltd	57-63 Princess Street Manchester M2 4EQ	(061) 236 5685
Equity & Law Unit Trust Managers Ltd	Amersham Road, High Wycombe Buckinghamshire HP13 5AL	(0494) 33377
F & C Unit Management Ltd	1 Laurence Pountney Hill London EC4R 0BA	(01) 623 4680
FS Investment Managers Ltd	190 West George Street Glasgow G2 2PA	(041) 332 6462
Fidelity International Management Ltd	25-26 Lovat Lane London EC3R 8LL	(01) 283 9911
Fielding Management Company Ltd	Garrard House, 31 Gresham Street London EC2V 7DX	(01) 606 7711
Framlington Unit Management Ltd	3 London Wall Buildings, London Wall London EC2M 5NQ	(01) 628 5181
Friends' Provident Unit Trust Managers Ltd	Pixham End, Dorking Surrey RH4 1QA	(0306) 885055
GAM Sterling Management Ltd	65 Holborn Viaduct London EC1A 2DR	(01) 248 4000
G & A Unit Trust Managers Ltd	5 Rayleigh Road Brentwood, Essex	(0277) 227300
GT Unit Managers	8th Floor, 8 Devonshire Square London EC2M 4YJ	(01) 283 2575
Gartmore Fund Managers Ltd	Cayzer House, St Mary Axe London EC3A 8BP	(01) 623 1212

Granville Unit Trust Management Ltd	8 Lovat Lane London EC3R 8DT	(01) 621 1212
Grofund Managers Ltd	Pinners Hall, 8-9 Austin Friars London EC2N 2AE	(01) 588 5317
Guardian Royal Exchange Unit Managers Ltd	Royal Exchange London EC3V 3LS	(01) 283 7101
Hambros Bank Unit Trust Managers Ltd	41 Bishopsgate London EC2P 2AA	(01) 588 2851
Henderson Unit Trust Management Ltd	26 Finsbury Square London EC2A 1DA	(01) 638 5757
Heritable Unit Trust Managers Ltd	52 Berkeley Square London W1X 6EH	(01) 493 6621
Hesmoss Unit Trust Managers Ltd	30-31 Friar Street, Reading Berkshire RG11AH	(0734) 595511
Hill Samuel Unit Trust Managers Ltd	45 Beech Street London EC2 2LX	(01) 628 8011
IBI Fund Managers Ltd	54 Pall Mall London SW1Y 5JH	(01) 222 1000
James Capel & Company Unit Trust Management Ltd	Winchester House, 100 Old Broad Street London EC2N 1BQ	(01) 588 6010
James Finlay Unit Trust Management Ltd	Finlay House, 10-14 West Nile Street Glasgow G1 2PP	(041) 204 1321
John Govett Unit Management Ltd	Winchester House, 77 London Wall London EC2N 1DH	(01) 588 5620
Key Fund Managers Ltd	14 Dominion Street London EC2H 2RJ	(061) 236 5685

Company Name	Address	Telephone No:
Kleinwort Benson Unit Managers Ltd	20 Fenchurch Street London EC3P 3DB	(01) 623 8000
L & C Unit Trust Management Ltd	The Stock Exchange London EC2N 1HA	(01) 588 2800
Lazard Brothers & Company Ltd	21 Moorfields London EC2P 2HT	(01) 588 2721
Legal & General (Unit Trust Managers) Ltd	Grosvenor House, 125 High Street Croydon, Surrey CR9 3UA	(01) 681 5177
Lloyds Bank Unit Trust Managers Ltd	Capital House, 1-5 Perrymount Road Haywards Heath, West Sussex RH16 3SP	(0444) 459144
London Law Unit Trust Management Ltd	Bailey House, Old Seacoal Lane Ludgate Hill, London EC4M 7LR	(01) 236 6105
London & Manchester Trust Management Ltd	Winslade Park Exeter EX5 1DS	(0392) 52155
M & G Securities Ltd	Three Quays, Tower Hill London EC3R 6BQ	(01) 626 4588
MGM Unit Managers Ltd	MGM House, Heene Road, Worthing West Sussex BN11 2DY	(0903) 204631
MLA Unit Trust Management Ltd	99-100 Sandling Road, Maidstone Kent ME14 1XX	(0622) 679351
Manulife Management Ltd	PO Box 21, Manulife House, St Georges Way Stevenage, Hertfordshire SG1 1HP	(0438) 356101
Marlborough Court Fund Managers Ltd	103 Oxford Street Manchester M60 7HA	(061) 236 9432

Martin Currie Investment Management Ltd	29 Charlotte Square Edinburgh EH2 2HA	(031) 225 3811
Mencap Unit Trust Managers Ltd	Unicorn House, 252 Romford Road London E7 9JB	(01) 534 5544
Mercury Fund Managers Ltd	33 King William Street London EC4R 9AS	(01) 280 2222
Midland Bank Group Unit Trust Managers Ltd	5th Floor, Courtwood House Silver Street Head, Sheffield S1 3RD	(0742) 79842/5
Minster Fund Managers Ltd	Minster House, Arthur Street London EC4R 9BH	(01) 623 1050
Montagu Unit Trust Managers Ltd	11 Devonshire Square London EC2M 4YR	(01) 626 3434
NFU Mutual Unit Managers Ltd	Tiddington Road Stratford-upon-Avon CV37 7BJ	(0789) 204211
National Provident Investment Managers Ltd	PO Box 227, 48 Gracechurch Street London EC3P 3HH	(01) 623 4200
Northgate Unit Trust Managers Ltd	3 London Wall Buildings London EC2M 5PU	(01) 638 1212
Norwich General Trust Ltd	12 Surrey Street Norwich NR1 3NJ	(0603) 622200
Octavian Unit Trust Managers Ltd	84 Fenchurch Street London EC3M 4BY	(01) 265 0371
Pearl Trust Managers Ltd	252 High Holborn London WC1V 7EB	(01) 405 8441
Perpetual Unit Trust Management Ltd	48 Hart Street, Henley-on-Thames Oxon RG9 2AZ	(0491) 576868

183

Company Name	Address	Telephone No:
Prudential Unit Trust Managers Ltd	Valentines House, 51-69 Ilford Hill Ilford, Essex IG1 2DJ	(01) 478 3377
Quilter Management Company Ltd	Garrard House, Gresham Street London EC2V 7LH	(01) 600 4177
Reliance Unit Managers Ltd	Reliance House, Tunbridge Wells Kent TN4 8BL	(0892) 22271
Rowan Unit Trust Management Ltd	1 Finsbury Avenue London EC2M 2PA	(01) 606 1066
Royal Life Fund Management Ltd	PO Box 30, New Hall Place Liverpool L69 3HS	(051) 227 4422
Royal London Unit Trust Managers Ltd (The)	Royal London House, Middleborough Colchester, Essex CO1 1RA	(0206) 44155
Royal Trust Company of Canada Fund Management Ltd (The)	Royal Trust House, 48-50 Cannon Street London EC4N 6LD	(01) 236 6044
Save & Prosper Securities Ltd	1 Finsbury Avenue London EC2M 2QY	(01) 588 1717
Schroder Unit Trust Managers Ltd	Regal House, 14 James Street London WC2 8BT	(01) 836 8731
Scottish Equitable Fund Managers Ltd	28 St Andrew Square Edinburgh EH2 1YF	(031) 556 9101
Scottish Mutual Investment Managers Ltd	109 St Vincent Street Glasgow G2 5HN	(041) 248 6321
Scottish Provident Investment Management Ltd	PO Box 58, 6 St Andrew Square Edinburgh EH2 2YA	(031) 556 9181

Scottish Unit Managers Ltd	29 Charlotte Square Edinburgh EH2 4HA	(031) 225 3811
Scottish Widows' Fund Management Ltd	15 Dalkeith Road Edinburgh EH16 5BX	(031) 655 6000
Standard Life Trust Management Ltd	PO Box 62, 3 George Street Edinburgh EH2 2XZ	(031) 225 7971
Stewart Unit Trust Managers Ltd	45 Charlotte Square Edinburgh EH2 4HW	(031) 226 3271
Sun Alliance Fund Management Ltd	Sun Alliance House, North Street Horsham, West Sussex RH12 1BT	(0403) 64141
Swiss Life Pension Trust Management Company Ltd	9-12 Cheapside London EC2V 6AL	(01) 236 3841
Target Trust Managers Ltd	7-9 Bream's Buildings London EC4A 1EU	(01) 831 8244
Target Trust Managers (Scotland) Ltd	19 Atholl Crescent Edinburgh EH3 8HQ	
Temple Bar Unit Trust Managers Ltd	Electra House, Temple Place Victoria Embankment, London WC2R 3HP	(01) 836 7766
Touche, Remnant Unit Trust Management Ltd	Mermaid House, 2 Puddle Dock London EC4V 3AT	(01) 236 6565
Trades Union Unit Trust Managers Ltd	100 Wood Street London EC2P 2AJ	(01) 628 8011
Transatlantic & General Securities Co Ltd	91-99 New London Road, Chelmsford Essex CM2 0PY	(0245) 51651
TSB Unit Trusts Ltd	PO Box 3, Keens House, Andover Hampshire SP10 1PG	(0264) 62188

Company Name	Address	Telephone No:
Tyndall Managers Ltd	18 Canynge Road Bristol BS99 7UA	(0272) 732241
Vanguard Trust Managers Ltd	Bath House, Holborn Viaduct London EC1A 2EU	(01) 236 5080
Wardley Unit Trust Managers Ltd	Wardley House, 7 Devonshire Square London EC2M 4HN	(01) 626 4411
Waverley Asset Management Ltd	13 Charlotte Square Edinburgh EH2 4DJ	(031) 225 1551

Source: Unit Trust Association

Section VI

The Association of Investment Trust Companies

– List of Members –

Name of Trust / Address / Tel. No.: / (Management)	Investment policy sector based on Investment Trust Table
Aberdeen Trust plc *(Aberdeen Fund Managers)* 9 Queen's Terrace, Aberdeen AB1 1XL. Tel: (0224) 631999	Income Growth
The Ailsa Investment Trust plc *(J. Rothschild Investment Management Ltd)* 66 St James's Street, London SW1A 1NE. Tel: (01) 493 8111	Special Features
The Alliance Trust plc *(Independent)* Meadow House, 64 Reform Street, Dundee DD1 1TJ. Tel: (0382) 21234	Capital & Income Growth
Altifund plc *(Gartmore Investment Management Ltd)* Cayzer House, 2 St Mary Axe, London EC3A 8BP. Tel: (01) 623 1212	Split Capital
The Alva Investment Trust plc *(Parsons Corporate Services Ltd)* PO Box 113, 100 West Nile Street, Glasgow G1 2QU. Tel: (041) 332 8791	Special Features
American Trust plc *(Edinburgh Fund Managers plc)* 4 Melville Crescent, Edinburgh EH3 7JB. Tel: (031) 226 4931	Capital Growth: North America
Anglo-American Securities Corp plc *(Morgan Grenfell & Co Ltd)* 72 London Wall, London EC2M 5NH. Tel: (01) 588 4545	Capital Growth: General
The Ashdown Investment Trust plc *(J. Henry Schroder Wagg & Co Ltd)* 36 Old Jewry Street, London EC2M 8BS. Tel: (01) 382 6000	Capital Growth: General

Name of Trust / Address / Tel. No: / (Management)	Investment policy sector based on Investment Trust Table
Atlantic Assets Trust plc *(Ivory & Sime plc)* 1 Charlotte Square, Edinburgh EH2 4DZ. Tel: (031) 225 1357	Capital Growth: General
The Baillie Gifford Japan Trust plc *(Baillie Gifford & Co)* 3 Glenfinlas Street, Edinburgh EH3 6YY. Tel: (031) 225 2581	Capital Growth: Japan
Baillie Gifford Technology plc *(Baillie Gifford & Co)* 3 Glenfinlas Street, Edinburgh EH3 6YY. Tel: (031) 225 2581	Capital Growth: Technology
The Bankers' Investment plc *(Touche Remnant & Co)* Mermaid House, 2 Puddle Dock, London EC2M 4YJ. Tel: (01) 236 6565	Capital & Income Growth
The Berry Trust plc *(GT Management Ltd)* 8th Floor, 8 Devonshire Square, London EC2M 7DJ. Tel: (01) 283 2575	Capital Growth: International
Bingham Investments Ltd* *(Independent)* Barrington House, Gresham Street, London EC2V 7HE. Tel: (01) 606 6474	
The Border & Southern Stockholders Trust plc *(John Govett & Co Ltd)* Winchester House, 77 London Wall, London EC2N 1DH. Tel: (01) 588 5620	Capital & Income Growth
British American & General Trust plc *(Kleinwort Benson Investment Management Ltd)* 20 Fenchurch Street, London EC3P 3DB. Tel: (01) 623 8000	Capital Growth: Technology
British Assets Trust plc *(Ivory & Sime plc)* 1 Charlotte Square, Edinburgh EH2 4DZ. Tel: (031) 225 1357	Income Growth
British Empire Securities & General Trust plc *(Laurentian Financial Services Ltd)* Imperial Life House, London Road, Guildford, Surrey GU1 1TA. Tel: (04835) 71255	Capital Growth General
The British Kidney Patient Association Investment Trust plc *(Henderson Admin. Ltd)* 26 Finsbury Square, London EC2A 1DA. Tel: (01) 638 5757	Capital & Income Growth
The Brunner Investment Trust plc *(Kleinwort Benson Investment Management Ltd)* 20 Fenchurch Street, London EC3P 3DB. Tel: (01) 623 8000	Capital & Income Growth

Candover Investments plc *(Independent)*
4-7 Red Lion Court, London EC4A 3EB. Tel: (01) 583 5090 — Special Features

The Charter Trust & Agency plc *(Kleinwort Benson Investment Management Ltd)*
20 Fenchurch Street, London EC3P 3DB. Tel: (01) 623 8000 — Capital & Income Growth

Charterhouse J. Rothschild Pacific Investment Trust plc
(J. Rothschild Charterhouse Management Ltd)
65 Holborn Viaduct, London EC1A 2DR. Tel: (01) 248 4000 — Capital Growth: Far East

Child Health Research Investment Trust plc
(J. Rothschild Investment Management Ltd)
65 Holborn Viaduct, London EC1A 2DR. Tel: (01) 493 8111 — Split Capital

City & Commercial Investment Trust plc *(Montagu Investment Management Ltd)*
11 Devonshire Square, London EC2M 4YR. Tel: (01) 626 3434 — Split Capital

City & Foreign Investment plc *(Montagu Investment Management Ltd)*
11 Devonshire Square, London EC2M 4YR. Tel: (01) 626 3434 — Capital Growth: Commodities and Energy

The City of Oxford Investment Trust plc *(Hambros Bank Ltd)*
51 Bishopsgate, London EC2P 2AA. Tel: (01) 588 2851 — Capital & Income Growth: United Kingdom

Consolidated Venture Trust plc *(Montagu Investment Management Ltd)*
11 Devonshire Square, London EC2M 4YR. Tel: (01) 626 3434 — Special Features

The Continental & Industrial Trust plc *(J. Henry Schroder Wagg & Co Ltd)*
36 Old Jewry, London EC2M 8BS. Tel: (01) 382 6000 — Capital & Income Growth

Crescent Japan Investment Trust plc *(Edinburgh Fund Managers plc)*
4 Melville Crescent, Edinburgh EH3 7JB. Tel: (031) 226 4931 — Capital Growth: Japan

Cystic Fibrosis Research Investment Trust plc *(Fidelity International Management Ltd)*
22 St Andrew Street, London EC4A 3AN. Tel: (01) 353 5691 — Split Capital

Drayton Consolidated Trust plc *(Montagu Investment Management Ltd)*
11 Devonshire Square, London EC2M 4YR. Tel: (01) 626 3434 — Special Features

Name of Trust / Address / Tel. No: / (Management)	Investment policy sector based on Investment Trust Table
Drayton Far Eastern Trust plc *(Montagu Investment Management Ltd)* 11 Devonshire Square, London EC2M 4YR. Tel: (01) 626 3434	Capital Growth: Far East
Drayton Japan Trust plc *(Montagu Investment Management Ltd)* 11 Devonshire Square, London EC2M 4YR. Tel: (01) 626 3434	Capital Growth: Japan
Drayton Premier Investment Trust plc *(Montagu Investment Management Ltd)* 11 Devonshire Square, London EC2M 4YR. Tel: (01) 626 3434	Income Growth
Dualvest plc *(Montagu Investment Management Ltd)* 11 Devonshire Square, London EC2M 4YR. Tel: (01) 626 3434	Split Capital
Dundee & London Investment Trust plc *(Tay & Thames Investment Services Ltd)* Belsize House, West Ferry, Dundee DD5 1NF. Tel: (0382) 78244	Smaller Companies
Edinburgh American Assets Trust plc *(Ivory & Sime plc)* 1 Charlotte Square, Edinburgh EH2 4DZ. Tel: (031) 225 1357	Capital Growth: North America
Edinburgh Financial Trust plc *(Stanecastle Assets Ltd)* 43 Charlotte Square, Edinburgh EH2 4HQ. Tel: (031) 225 7685	Special Features
The Edinburgh Investment Trust plc *(Dunedin Fund Managers Ltd)* 3 Charlotte Square, Edinburgh EH2 4DS. Tel: (031) 225 4571	Capital & Income Growth
Electra Investment Trust plc *(Electra House Group)* Electra House, Temple Place, Victoria Embankment, London WC2R 3HP. Tel: (01) 836 7766	Special Features
Electric & General Investment Company plc *(Henderson Administration Ltd)* 26 Finsbury Square, London EC2A 1DA. Tel: (01) 638 5757	Capital Growth: General
English & International Trust plc *(Montagu Investment Management Ltd)* 11 Devonshire Square, London EC2M 4YR. Tel: (01) 626 3434	Smaller Companies
The English & New York Trust plc *(Kleinwort Benson Investment Management Ltd)* 20 Fenchurch Street, London EC3P 3DB. Tel: (01) 623 8000	Capital Growth: International

English & Scottish Investors plc *(Gartmore Investment Management Ltd)*
Cayzer House, 2 St Mary Axe, London EC3A 8BP. Tel: (01) 623 1212 — Capital Growth: International

English National Investment Company plc *(Henderson Administration Ltd)*
26 Finsbury Square, London EC2A 1DA. Tel: (01) 638 5757 — Split Capital

Equity Consort Investment Trust plc *(N. M. Rothschild Asset Management Ltd)*
PO Box 185, New Court, St Swithin's Lane, London EC4P 4DU. Tel: (01) 280 5000 — Split Capital

F & C Alliance Investment plc *(Foreign & Colonial Management Ltd)*
1 Laurence Pountney Hill, London EC4R 0BA. Tel: (01) 623 4680 — Smaller Companies

F & C Enterprise Trust plc *(Foreign & Colonial Management Ltd)*
1 Laurence Pountney Hill, London EC4R 0BA. Tel: (01) 623 4680 — Special Features

F & C Eurotrust plc *(Foreign & Colonial Management Ltd)*
1 Laurence Pountney Hill, London EC4R 0BA. Tel: (01) 623 4680 — Capital Growth: International

F & C Pacific Investment Trust plc *(Foreign & Colonial Management Ltd)*
1 Laurence Pountney Hill, London EC4R 0BA. Tel: (01) 623 4680 — Capital Growth: Far East

The Family Investment Trust plc *(Kleinwort Benson Investment Management Ltd)*
20 Fenchurch Street, London EC3P 3DB. Tel: (01) 623 8000 — Smaller Companies

First Charlotte Assets Trust plc *(Ivory & Sime plc)*
1 Charlotte Square, Edinburgh EH2 4DZ. Tel: (031) 225 1357 — Smaller Companies

The First Scottish American Trust plc *(Dunedin Fund Managers Ltd)*
Belsize House, West Ferry, Dundee DD5 1NF. Tel: (0382) 78244 — Income Growth

The Fleming American Investment Trust plc *(R. Fleming Invest. Management Ltd)*
P & O Building (2nd Floor), 122 Leadenhall Street,
London EC3V 4QR. Tel: (01) 638 5858 — Capital Growth: North America

The Fleming Claverhouse Investment Trust plc *(R. Fleming Invest. Management Ltd)*
P & O Building (2nd Floor), 122 Leadenhall Street,
London EC3V 4QR. Tel: (01) 638 5858 — Capital & Income Growth: United Kingdom

Name of Trust / Address / Tel. No: / (Management)	Investment policy sector based on Investment Trust Table
The Fleming Enterprise Investment Trust plc *(R. Fleming Invest. Management Ltd)* P & O Building (2nd Floor), 122 Leadenhall Street, London EC3V 4QR. Tel: (01) 638 5858	Special Features
The Fleming Far Eastern Investment Trust plc *(R. Fleming Invest. Management Ltd)* P & O Building (2nd Floor), 122 Leadenhall Street, London EC3V 4QR. Tel: (01) 638 5858	Capital Growth: Far East
The Fleming Fledgeling Investment Trust plc *(R. Fleming Invest. Management Ltd)* P & O Building (2nd Floor), 122 Leadenhall Street, London EC3V 4QR. Tel: (01) 638 5858	Smaller Companies
The Fleming Japanese Investment Trust plc *(R. Fleming Invest. Management Ltd)* P & O Building (2nd Floor), 122 Leadenhall Street, London EC3V 4QR. Tel: (01) 638 5858	Capital Growth: Japan
The Fleming Mercantile Investment Trust plc *(R. Fleming Invest. Management Ltd)* P & O Building (2nd Floor), 122 Leadenhall Street, London EC3V 4QR. Tel: (01) 638 5858	Special Features
The Fleming Overseas Investment Trust plc *(R. Fleming Invest. Management Ltd)* P & O Building (2nd Floor), 122 Leadenhall Street, London EC3V 4QR. Tel: (01) 638 5858	Capital Growth: International
The Fleming Technology Investment Trust plc *(R. Fleming Invest. Management Ltd)* P & O Building (2nd Floor), 122 Leadenhall Street, London EC3V 4QR. Tel: (01) 638 5858	Capital Growth: Technology
The Fleming Universal Investment Trust plc *(R. Fleming Invest. Management Ltd)* P & O Building (2nd Floor), 122 Leadenhall Street, London EC3V 4QR. Tel: (01) 638 5858	Capital Growth: International
The Foreign & Colonial Investment Trust plc *(Foreign & Colonial Management Ltd)* 1 Laurence Pountney Hill, London EC4R 0BA. Tel: (01) 623 4680	Capital & Income Growth

Fundinvest plc *(Montagu Investment Management Ltd)*
11 Devonshire Square, London EC2M 4YR. Tel: (01) 626 3434 — Split Capital

GT Global Recovery Investment Trust plc *(GT Management Ltd)*
8th Floor, 8 Devonshire Square, London EC2M 4YJ. Tel: (01) 283 2575 — Special Features

GT Japan Investment Trust plc *(GT Management Ltd)*
8th Floor, 8 Devonshire Square, London EC2M 4YJ. Tel: (01) 283 2575 — Capital Growth: Japan

Gartmore American Securities plc *(Gartmore Investment Management Ltd)*
Cayzer House, 2 St Mary Axe, London EC3A 8BP. Tel: (01) 623 1212 — Capital Growth: North America

Gartmore Information & Financial Trust plc *(Gartmore Investment Management Ltd)*
Cayzer House, 2 St Mary Axe, London EC3A 8BP. Tel: (01) 623 1212 — Capital Growth: International

General Consolidated Investment Trust plc *(Philip Hill (Management) Ltd)*
1 Brewer's Green, Buckingham Gate, London SW1H 0RB. Tel: (01) 222 4393 — Capital & Income Growth

The General Funds Investment Trust plc *(City Financial Administration Ltd)*
Regis House, King William Street, London EC4R 9AR. Tel: (01) 623 4951 — Capital Growth: International

The General Stockholders Investment Trust plc *(John Govett & Co Ltd)*
Winchester House, 77 London Wall, London EC2N 1DH. Tel: (01) 588 5620 — Smaller Companies

Glasgow Stockholders Trust plc *(Gartmore Investment (Scotland) Ltd)*
Ashley House, 181-195 West George Street, Glasgow G2 2HB. Tel: (041) 248 3972 — Smaller Companies

Globe Investment Trust plc *(Electra House Group)*
Electra House, Temple Place, Victoria Embankment
London WC2R 3HP. Tel: (01) 836 7766 — Capital & Income Growth

Greenfriar Investment Company plc *(Henderson Administration Ltd)*
26 Finsbury Square, London EC2A 1DA. Tel: (01) 638 5757 — Capital Growth: General

Group Investors plc *(CS Investments Ltd)*
125 High Holborn, London WC1V 6PY. Tel: (01) 242 1148 — Capital Growth: International

Hambros Investment Trust plc *(Hambros Bank Ltd)*
51 Bishopsgate, London EC2P 2AA. Tel: (01) 588 2851 — Capital Growth: International

Name of Trust / Address / Tel. No: / (Management)	Investment policy sector based on Investment Trust Table
Philip Hill Investment Trust plc *(Philip Hill Management Ltd)* 1 Brewer's Green, Buckingham Gate, London SW1H 0RB. Tel: (01) 222 4393	Capital & Income Growth
The Independent Investment Company plc *(Ivory & Sime plc)* 1 Charlotte Square, Edinburgh EH2 4DZ. Tel: (031) 225 1357	Capital Growth: Technology
'Investing in Success' Equities plc *(City Financial Administration Ltd)* Regis House, King William Street, London EC4R 9AR. Tel: (01) 623 4951	Capital Growth: International
Investors Capital Trust plc *(Independent)* 9 Charlotte Square, Edinburgh EH2 4DY. Tel: (031) 225 4533	Capital Growth: International
Japan Assets Trust plc *(Ivory & Sime plc)* 1 Charlotte Square, Edinburgh EH2 4DZ. Tel: (031) 225 1357	Capital Growth: Japan
Jersey General Investment Trust Ltd* *(Independent)* PO Box 1, 21 Broad Street, St Helier, Jersey. Tel: (0534) 31541	Capital & Income Growth
Jos Holdings plc *(Kleinwort Benson Investment Management Ltd)* 20 Fenchurch Street, London EC3P 3DB. Tel: (01) 623 8000	Capital & Income Growth
Keystone Investment Company plc *(Warburg Investment Management Ltd)* 33 King William Street, London EC4R 9AS. Tel: (01) 280 2222	Capital & Income Growth
Lake View Investment Trust plc *(John Govett & Co Ltd)* Winchester House, 77 London Wall, London EC2N 1DH. Tel: (01) 588 5620	Capital Growth: Far East
Lancashire & London Investment Trust plc *(Rea Brothers plc)* Alderman's House, Alderman's Walk, London EC2M 3XR. Tel: (01) 623 1155	Capital & Income Growth
The Law Debenture Corporation Ltd *(Independent)* Estates House, 66 Gresham Street, London EC2V 7HX. Tel: (01) 606 5451	Capital & Income Growth
London & Gartmore Investment Trust plc *(Gartmore Investment Management Ltd)* Cayzer House, 2 St Mary Axe, London EC3A 8BP. Tel: (01) 623 1212	Capital Growth: International

London & Strathclyde Trust plc *(Gartmore Investment Management Ltd)*
Cayzer House, 2 St Mary Axe, London EC3A 8BP. Tel: (01) 623 1212 — Capital & Income Growth

London Atlantic Investment Trust plc *(Investors in Industry Portfolio Management Ltd)*
91 Waterloo Road, London SE1 8XP. Tel: (01) 928 7822 — Smaller Companies

London Trust plc *(London Trust Management Services Ltd)*
15 Southampton Place, London WC1A 2BU. Tel: (01) 242 2224 — Special Features

Lowland Investment Company plc *(Henderson Administration Ltd)*
26 Finsbury Square, London EC2A 1DA. Tel: (01) 638 5757 — Income Growth

Marine Adventure Sailing Trust plc *(J. Rothschild Investment Management)*
65 Holborn Viaduct, London   EC1A 2DR. Tel: (01) 248 4000 — Split Capital

Meldrum Investment Trust plc *(Gartmore Investment Management Ltd)*
Cayzer House, 2 St Mary Axe, London EC3A 8BP. Tel: (01) 623 1212 — Capital & Income Growth

The Merchants Trust plc *(Kleinwort Benson Investment Management Ltd)*
20 Fenchurch Street, London EC3P 3DB. Tel: (01) 623 8000 — Income Growth

Mid Wynd International Investment Trust plc *(Baillie Gifford & Co)*
3 Glenfinlas Street, Edinburgh EH3 6YY. Tel: (031) 225 2581 — Capital Growth: International

The Monks Investment Trust plc *(Baillie Gifford & Co)*
3 Glenfinlas Street, Edinburgh EH3 6YY. Tel: (031) 225 2581 — Capital Growth: International

Moorgate Investment Trust plc *(Philip Hill (Management) Ltd)*
1 Brewer's Green, Buckingham Gate, London SW1H 0RB. Tel: (01) 222 4393 — Smaller Companies

Murray Growth Investment Trust plc *(Murray Johnstone Ltd)*
163 Hope Street, Glasgow G2 2UH. Tel: (041) 221 5521 — Capital Growth: International

Murray Income Trust plc *(Murray Johnstone Ltd)*
163 Hope Street, Glasgow G2 2UH. Tel: (041) 221 5521 — Income Growth

Murray International Investment Trust plc *(Murray Johnstone Ltd)*
163 Hope Street, Glasgow G2 2UH. Tel: (041) 221 5521 — Income Growth

195

Name of Trust / Address / Tel. No.: / (Management)	Investment policy sector based on Investment Trust Table
Murray Smaller Markets Trust plc *(Murray Johnstone Ltd)* 163 Hope Street, Glasgow G2 2UH. Tel: (041) 221 5521	Capital Growth: International
Murray Ventures plc *(Murray Johnstone Ltd)* 163 Hope Street, Glasgow G2 2UH. Tel: (041) 221 5521	Special Features
New Australia Investment Trust plc *(Edinburgh Fund Managers plc)* 4 Melville Crescent, Edinburgh EH3 7JB. Tel: (031) 226 4931	Capital Growth: Far East
New Court Trust plc *(N. M. Rothschild Asset Management Ltd)* PO Box 185, New Court, St Swithin's Lane, London EC4P 4DU. Tel: (01) 280 5000	Capital & Income Growth: United Kingdom
New Darien Oil Trust plc *(Hodgson Martin)* 4a St Andrew Square, Edinburgh EH2 2BD. Tel: (031) 557 3560	Capital Growth: Commodities & Energy
The New Throgmorton Trust (1983) plc *(Throgmorton Investment Management Services Ltd)* Royal London House, 22–25 Finsbury Square, London EC2A 1DS. Tel: (01) 638 0317	Split Capital
New Tokyo Investment Trust plc *(Edinburgh Fund Managers plc)* 4 Melville Crescent, Edinburgh EH3 7JB. Tel: (031) 226 4931	Capital Growth: Japan
The Nineteen Twenty Eight Investment Trust plc *(London & Manchester)* Imperial House, Dominion Street, London EC2M 2SP. Tel: (01) 628 8000	Special Features
North Atlantic Securities Corp plc *(Morgan Grenfell & Co Ltd)* 72 London Wall, London EC2M 5NH. Tel: (01) 588 4545	Capital Growth: International
The North British Canadian Investment Company plc *(Investors in Industry Portfolio Management Ltd)* 29 Charlotte Square, Edinburgh EH2 4HA. Tel: (031) 225 3811	Smaller Companies
North Sea Assets plc *(Ivory & Sime plc)* 1 Charlotte Square, Edinburgh EH2 4DZ. Tel: (031) 225 1357	Capital Growth: Commodities & Energy

The Northern American Trust plc *(Dunedin Fund Managers Ltd)*
Belsize House, West Ferry, Dundee DD5 1NF. Tel: (0382) 78244 — Capital Growth: International

The Northern Securities Trust plc *(GT Management Ltd)*
8th Floor, 8 Devonshire Square, London EC2M 4YJ. Tel: (01) 283 2575 — Capital Growth: International

Outwich Investment Trust plc *(Baring Brothers & Co Ltd)*
8 Bishopsgate, London EC2N 4AE. Tel: (01) 283 8833 — Capital & Income Growth

Pacific Assets Trust plc *(Ivory & Sime plc)*
1 Charlotte Square, Edinburgh EH2 4DZ. Tel: (031) 225 1357 — Capital Growth: Far East

Personal Assets Trust plc *(Ivory & Sime plc)*
1 Charlotte Square, Edinburgh EH2 4DZ. Tel: (031) 225 1357 — Capital Growth: General

The Plantation Trust Company plc *(David Hume Investment Management Ltd)*
Empire House, 123 Kennington Road, London SE11 6SF. Tel: (01) 582 4174 — Capital Growth: Commodities & Energy

Precious Metals Trust plc *(J. Rothschild Investment Management Ltd)*
66 St James's Street, London SW1A 1NE. Tel: (01) 493 8111 — Capital & Income Growth

Raeburn Investment Trust plc *(Lazard Securities Ltd)*
21 Moorfields, London EC2P 2HT. Tel: (01) 588 2721 — Split Capital

Rights & Issues Investment Trust plc *(Equity Finance Trust Holdings plc)*
Dauntsey House, Frederick's Place, Old Jewry, London EC2R 8HN. Tel: (01) 606 2167 — Capital & Income Growth

River & Mercantile Trust plc *(Tarbutt & Co Ltd)*
7 Lincoln's Inn Fields, London WC2A 3BP. Tel: (01) 405 7722 — Capital & Income Growth

The River Plate & General Investment Trust plc *(Tarbutt & Co Ltd)*
7 Lincoln's Inn Fields, London WC2A 3BP. Tel: (01) 405 7722 — Capital Growth: International

Romney Trust plc *(Lazard Securities Ltd)*
21 Moorfields, London EC2P 2HT. Tel: (01) 588 2721 — Smaller Companies

St Andrew Trust plc *(Martin Currie & Co)*
29 Charlotte Square, Edinburgh EH2 4HA. Tel: (031) 225 3811

Name of Trust / Address / Tel. No: / (Management)	Investment policy sector based on Investment Trust Table
Save & Prosper Linked Investment Trust plc *(Save & Prosper Group Ltd)* 1 Finsbury Avenue, London EC2M 2QY. Tel: (01) 588 1717	Split Capital
Save & Prosper Return of Assets Investment Trust plc *(Save & Prosper Group Ltd)* 1 Finsbury Avenue, London EC2M 2QY. Tel: (01) 588 1717	Capital & Income Growth
The Scottish & Mercantile Investment plc *(Rea Brothers plc)* Alderman's House, Alderman's Walk, London EC2M 3XR. Tel: (01) 623 1155	Capital & Income Growth
The Scottish American Investment Company plc *(Stewart Fund Managers Ltd)* 45 Charlotte Square, Edinburgh EH2 4HW.. Tel: (031) 226 3271	Smaller Companies
Scottish Cities Investment Trust plc *(Rea Brothers plc)* Alderman's House, Alderman's Walk, London EC2M 3XR. Tel: (01) 623 1155	Capital & Income Growth
The Scottish Eastern Investment Trust plc *(Martin Currie & Co)* 29 Charlotte Square, Edinburgh EH2 4HA. Tel: (031) 225 3811	Capital Growth: International
The Scottish Investment Trust plc *(Independent)* 6 Albyn Place, Edinburgh EH2 4NL. Tel: (031) 225 7781	Capital Growth: International
The Scottish Mortgage & Trust plc *(Baillie Gifford & Co)* 3 Glenfinlas Street, Edinburgh EH3 6YY. Tel: (031) 225 2581	Capital & Income Growth
The Scottish National Trust plc *(Gartmore Investment (Scotland) Ltd)* Ashley House, 181-195 West George Street, Glasgow G2 2HB. Tel: (041) 248 3972	Capital & Income Growth
Scottish Northern Investment Trust plc *(Paull & Williamsons)* Investment House, PO Box 65, 6 Union Row, Aberdeen AB9 8DQ. Tel: (0224) 631414	Capital & Income Growth
The Second Alliance Trust plc *(Independent)* 64 Reform Street, Dundee DD1 1TJ. Tel: (0382) 21234	Capital & Income Growth
Securities Trust of Scotland plc *(Martin Currie & Co)* 29 Charlotte Square, Edinburgh EH2 4HA. Tel: (031) 225 3811	Income Growth

Shires Investment plc *(Stanecastle Assets Ltd)*
70 Finsbury Pavement, London EC2A 1SX. Tel: (01) 638 2777

Capital & Income Growth:
United Kingdom

The Smaller Companies International Trust plc *(Edinburgh Fund Managers)*
4 Melville Crescent, Edinburgh EH3 7JB. Tel: (031) 226 4931

Smaller Companies

Stewart Enterprise Investment Company plc *(Stewart Fund Managers Ltd)*
45 Charlotte Square, Edinburgh EH2 4HW. Tel: (031) 226 3271

Special Features

The Stockholders Investment Trust plc *(John Govett & Co Ltd)*
Winchester House, 77 London Wall, London EC2N 1DH. Tel: (01) 588 5620

Capital Growth: North America

TR Australia Investment Trust plc *(Touche Remnant & Co)*
Mermaid House, 2 Puddle Dock, London EC4V 3AT. Tel: (01) 236 6565

Capital Growth: Far East

TR City of London Trust plc *(Touche Remnant & Co)*
Mermaid House, 2 Puddle Dock, London EC4V 3AT. Tel: (01) 236 6565

Capital & Income Growth:
United Kingdom

TR Industrial & General Trust plc *(Touche Remnant & Co)*
Mermaid House, 2 Puddle Dock, London EC4V 3AT. Tel: (01) 236 6565

Capital & Income Growth

TR Natural Resources Investment Trust plc *(Touche Remnant & Co)*
Mermaid House, 2 Puddle Dock, London EC4V 3AT. Tel: (01) 236 6565

Capital Growth:
Commodities & Energy

TR North America Investment Trust plc *(Touche Remnant & Co)*
Mermaid House, 2 Puddle Dock, London EC4V 3AT. Tel: (01) 236 6565

Capital Growth: North America

TR Pacific Basin Investment Trust plc *(Touche Remnant & Co)*
Mermaid House, 2 Puddle Dock, London EC4V 3AT. Tel: (01) 236 6565

Capital Growth: Far East

TR Property Investment Trust plc *(Touche Remnant & Co)*
Mermaid House, 2 Puddle Dock, London EC4V 3AT. Tel: (01) 236 6565

Special Features

TR Technology Investment Trust plc *(Touche Remnant & Co)*
Mermaid House, 2 Puddle Dock, London EC4V 3AT. Tel: (01) 236 6565

Capital Growth: Technology

TR Trustees Corporation plc *(Touche Remnant & Co)*
Mermaid House, 2 Puddle Dock, London EC4V 3AT. Tel: (01) 236 6565

Smaller Companies

Name of Trust / Address / Tel. No: / (Management)	Investment policy sector based on Investment Trust Table
Temple Bar Investment Trust plc *(Electra House Group)* Electra House, Temple Place, Victoria Embankment, London WC2R 3HP. Tel: (01) 836 7766	Capital & Income Growth: United Kingdom
The Throgmorton Secured Growth Trust plc *(Throgmorton Investment Management Services Ltd)* Royal London House, 22-25 Finsbury Square, London EC2A 1DS. Tel: (01) 638 0317	Split Capital
The Throgmorton Trust plc *(Throgmorton Investment Management Services Ltd)* Royal London House, 22-25 Finsbury Square, London EC2A 1DS. Tel: (01) 638 0317	Smaller Companies
The Trans-Oceanic Trust plc *(J. Henry Schroder Wagg & Company Ltd)* 36 Old Jewry, London EC2R 8BS. Tel: (01) 382 6000	Capital Growth: International
Tribune Investment Trust plc *(Baring Brothers & Company Ltd)* 8 Bishopsgate, London EC2N 4AE. Tel: (01) 283 8833	Capital Growth: International
Triplevest plc *(Montagu Investment Management Ltd)* 11 Devonshire Square, London EC2M 4YR. Tel: (01) 626 3434	Split Capital
Trust of Property Shares plc *(Independent)* 6 Welbeck Street, London W1M 8BS. Tel: (01) 486 4684	Special Features
The United States Debenture Corporation plc *(GT Management Ltd)* 8th Floor, 8 Devonshire Square, London EC2M 4YJ. Tel: (01) 283 2575	Capital Growth: International
Updown Investment Company plc *(Independent)* 12 Tokenhouse Yard, London EC2R 7AN. Tel: (01) 588 2828	Capital Growth: General
Viking Resources Trust plc *(Ivory & Sime plc)* 1 Charlotte Square, Edinburgh EH2 4DZ. Tel: (031) 225 1357	Capital Growth: Commodities & Energy
The Wemyss Investment Trust plc *(Edinburgh Fund Managers Ltd)* 4 Melville Crescent, Edinburgh EH3 7JB. Tel: (031) 226 4931	Capital Growth: Commodities & Energy

Western Reversion Trust Ltd * *(Independent)*
79 Mount Street, London W1Y 5HJ. Tel: (01) 409 1785

The Winterbottom Energy Trust plc *(Baillie Gifford & Company)*
3 Glenfinlas Street, Edinburgh EH3 6YY. Tel: (031) 225 2581

Capital Growth:
Commodities & Energy

Witan Investment Company plc *(Henderson Administration Ltd)*
26 Finsbury Square, London EC2A 1DA. Tel: (01) 638 5757

Capital & Income Growth

Yeoman Investment Trust plc *(Independent)*
1 Brewer's Green, Buckingham Gate, London SW1H 0RB. Tel: (01) 222 4393

Capital & Income Growth

Total Number of Members = 167

* Indicates Company is not approved for taxation purposes.

Source: Association of Investment Trust Companies.

Section VII
Best of British
Top 100 Quoted Companies

COMPANY	MARKET VALUE £m	ACTIVITY	TELEPHONE: HEAD OFFICE
British Telecom	13,500.0*	Telecommunications.	(01) 356 5000
British Petroleum	9,551.2	Oil and natural gas.	(01) 920 8000
Shell Transport & Trading Company	7,546.1	Oil, natural gas and chemicals.	(01) 934 1234
Glaxo Holdings	4,866.7	Pharmaceuticals.	(01) 493 4060
Imperial Chemical Industries	4,794.0	General chemicals, petrochemicals and pharmaceuticals.	(01) 834 4444
BAT Industries	4,744.3	Holding company with diverse interests, including insurance, tobacco and retailing.	(01) 222 7979
General Electric Company	4,628.4	International producers of electrical equipment.	(01) 493 8484
BTR	3,929.7	Industrial rubber and fluid power transmission.	(01) 834 3848
Marks & Spencer	3,537.2	Retailers.	(01) 935 4422
Hanson Trust	2,872.6	Industrial and food products.	(01) 589 7070
Barclays	2,612.5	Banking.	(01) 626 1567
Beecham Group	2,566.3	Toiletries and pharmaceuticals.	(01) 560 5151

Company	Value	Description	Phone
National Westminster Bank	2,395.5	Banking.	(01) 726 1000
Cable & Wireless	2,385.0	International telecommunications.	(01) 242 4433
Grand Metropolitan	2,208.6	Hotels, brewing and gaming clubs.	(01) 629 7488
Sainsbury J.	2,198.2	Retailer, food and household goods.	(01) 921 6000
Prudential Corporation	2,115.6	Insurance.	(01) 405 9222
Great Universal Stores	2,023.0	Mail order, retailer, property and travel.	(01) 628 8011
Unilever	1,802.0	Branded consumer goods.	(051) 645 2000
Rio Tinto Zinc	1,790.0	Mining and chemicals.	(01) 930 2399
Bass	1,777.4	Brewery and leisure.	(01) 637 5499
Royal Insurance	1,592.1	Insurance.	(01) 283 4300
Land Securities	1,429.5	Property.	(01) 353 4222
BL	1,412.1	Motor manufacturers.	(01) 486 6000
Imperial Group	1,408.3	Tobacco.	(01) 235 7010
Lloyds Bank	1,401.0	Banking.	(01) 625 1500
Boots	1,391.9	Retail chemists.	(0602) 506111
Allied Lyons	1,315.7	Brewer and foods.	(01) 253 9911
Associated Dairies	1,248.9	Dairy goods and carpets.	(0532) 440141
Trafalgar House	1,243.9	Varied, including property, hotels and shipping.	(01) 499 9020
Sears Holdings	1,168.6	Retailers.	(01) 408 1180
BOC Group	1,156.4	Industrial gas producer.	(01) 748 2020
Legal and General	1,151.9	Insurance.	(01) 248 9678
Guardian Royal Exchange	1,135.2	Insurance.	(01) 283 7101

COMPANY	MARKET VALUE £m	ACTIVITY	TELEPHONE: HEAD OFFICE
Britoil	1,081.9	Oil.	(041) 204 2525
Trusthouse Forte	1,060.1	Hotels, catering.	(01) 437 7788
Distillers	1,056.8	Spirits.	(031) 337 7373
Reuters	1,053.3	International news organisation.	(01) 250 1122
General Accident	1,039.1	Insurance.	(0738) 21202
Tesco	1,016.6	Retailer.	(0992) 32222
Racal Electronic	1,015.4	Electronics.	(0344) 3244
Consolidated Goldfields	986.5	Mining.	(01) 606 1020
Dee Corporation	932.5	Retailer.	(0908) 607171
Plessey	928.2	Telecommunications, electronics and aerospace.	(01) 478 3040
Tarmac	921.3	Builders and engineers.	(0902) 41101
Thorn EMI	920.4	Electronics.	(01) 836 2444
Commercial Union	903.7	Insurance.	(01) 283 7500
Sun Alliance & London Insurance	903.2	Insurance.	(01) 588 2345
Burton Group	886.7	Retailer.	(0532) 494949
Associated British Foods	878.1	Manufacture and distributors of food.	(01) 589 6363
Peninsular & Oriental Steam Navigation Company	876.3	Shipping.	(01) 283 8000
Whitbread & Co	871.0	Brewer.	(01) 606 4455
Sedgwick Group	870.7	Insurance brokers.	(01) 377 3456

Company	Value	Description	Telephone
Hawker Siddeley	853.3	Aircraft, engineering.	(01) 930 6177
Fisons	842.3	Horticultural products, medicines and scientific equipment.	(0473) 56721
Midland Bank	830.1	Banking.	(01) 606 9911
Cadbury Schweppes	822.8	Confectionary, food, beverages.	(01) 262 1212
Standard Telephone & Cables	797.3	Telecommunications.	(01) 836 8055
Reckitt & Colman	793.1	Manufacturers of food, toiletries, pharmaceuticals and leisure products.	(01) 994 6464
Reed International	775.0	Publishing, paper and building products.	(01) 499 4020
British Aerospace	746.1	Aircraft and weapons.	(01) 930 1020
United Biscuits	739.3	Food.	(01) 560 3131
Smith & Nephew	737.5	Pharmaceuticals, toiletries and textiles.	(01) 836 7922
Royal Bank of Scotland	730.4	Banking.	(031) 556 8555
Standard Chartered Bank	721.5	Banking.	(01) 623 7500
Pearson	707.9	Merchant banking, publishing, leisure and oil services.	(01) 828 9020
Rank Organisation	686.8	Holding company with diverse interests, including cinema, business equipment and charter airways.	(01) 629 7454
Rowntree Mackintosh	662.5	Confectionery and grocery products.	(0904) 53071
Dixons Group	656.4	Holding company with diverse interests, including photographic, property and electronic.	(01) 952 2345
Hambro Life	644.5	Insurance.	(0793) 28291
Woolworth Holdings	636.5	Retailer.	(01) 262 1222
British Electric Traction	634.4	Diversified service company.	(01) 629 8886

COMPANY	MARKET VALUE £m	ACTIVITY	TELEPHONE: HEAD OFFICE
Argyll Group	624.0	Food retailer and manufacturer.	(01) 848 3801
Pilkington Group	623.3	Glass and glass fibre manufacturer.	(0744) 28882
Blue Circle Industries	618.7	Cement and building materials.	(01) 828 3456
British Home Stores	617.1	Retailer.	(01) 262 3288
Redland	596.0	Building materials.	(07372) 42488
MEPC	590.2	Property.	(01) 491 5300
MFI Furniture	587.0	Furniture and property.	(01) 903 1366
Ultramar	586.9	Oil company.	(01) 726 4545
News International	568.2	Publishing.	(01) 353 3030
Willis Faber	564.3	Insurance broker.	(01) 488 8111
Guest, Keen & Nettlefields	549.4	Engineering.	(0527) 23400
Guinness	543.3	Brewery holding company.	(01) 965 7700
Debenhams	539.7	Retailers and finance company.	(01) 408 4444
Courtaulds	527.3	Textiles.	(01) 629 9080
Hammerson Property	517.6	Property.	(01) 629 9494
Jaguar	516.6	Luxury motor cars.	(0203) 402121
Sun Life Assurance	513.0	Insurance.	(01) 606 7788
Harrisons & Crosfield	512.8	Commodities, shipping and finance.	(01) 626 4333
Ferranti	503.5	Engineering.	(061) 428 3644
Northern Foods	499.3	Dairy, meat products and brewing.	(0482) 25432

Company	Size (£m)	Activity	Telephone
English China Clays	478.4	Building materials.	(0726) 4482
Exco International	478.3	Financial services.	(01) 626 2483
BPB Industries	475.3	Building materials, electronics and paper products.	(0753) 73273
Ladbroke Group	465.9	Hotels, property and leisure.	(01) 459 8031
Bank of Scotland	465.5	Banking.	(031) 229 2555
Granada Group	454.6	Television and leisure.	(01) 734 8080
Coats Paton	451.0	Textiles.	(0417 221 8711
Lonrho	448.0	International trader.	(017 606 9898

NOTES:

1. The figures on company size refer to 12th June 1985. Fluctuations in share prices will alter the market value of companies.

2. The telephone number of the head office is supplied so potential investors can ring the company secretary for the latest report and accounts.

3. Many companies are simply holding groups with diverse interests. The description under 'activity' is designed to give a broad indication of the groups main operating area.

* Assumes shares fully paid-up. Partly paid £5,572.2m.